iCloud Standard Guide

Get to grips with managing your Apple devices and content, easily and automatically with iCloud

Andri Yadi

Fauzan Alfi

PUBLISHING

BIRMINGHAM - MUMBAI

iCloud Standard Guide

First published: November 2013

Production Reference: 1111113

Published by Packt Publishing Ltd.
Livery Place
35 Livery Street
Birmingham B3 2PB, UK.

ISBN 978-1-78216-050-2

www.packtpub.com

Cover Image by Prashant Timappa Shetty (sparkling.spectrum.123@gmail.com)

Credits

Authors

Andri Yadi

Fauzan Alfi

Reviewers

Daniel Mühlbachler

Sergio Martínez-Losa Del Rincón

Acquisition Editors

Usha Iyer

Sam Wood

Commissioning Editors

Shaon Basu

Nikhil Chinnari

Technical Editors

Siddhi Rane

Tarunveer Shetty

Copy Editors

Roshni Banerjee

Brandt D'Mello

Dipti Kapadia

Sayanee Mukherjee

Project Coordinator

Aboli Ambardekar

Proofreader

Simran Bhogal

Indexers

Rekha Nair

Priya Subramani

Production Coordinator

Kyle Albuquerque

Cover Work

Kyle Albuquerque

About the Authors

Andri Yadi is a developer, entrepreneur, influencer, and educator in the IT industry, especially in the mobile apps field.

As a developer, he has been developing in many well-known programming languages for the past 16 years. Since iOS SDK was first released in 2008, he's one of the early adopters in developing iOS apps with iOS SDK and Objective-C. He has developed more than 50 web and desktop apps and 10 iOS apps. He's the creator of a well-known iOS app in Indonesia, Movreak that is a social app for movies and the cinema.

As an entrepreneur, he has founded four software companies since 2003. The more recent one is PT. Dycode Cominfotech Development (DyCode), where he has been putting all his heart, time, thoughts, and passion for the last 6 years.

As an influencer, he has been actively influencing the mobile apps industry as well as the startup and developer community in Indonesia. He co-founded four developer communities; one of them is the ID-Objective-C community, Indonesia's first and biggest iOS developer community, where he also serves as the President. For his technical expertise and community influence, he has been awarded the Microsoft Most Valuable Professional (MVP) award for 6 years in a row. He occasionally shares his thoughts on his blog http://andriyadi.me.

As an educator, he has delivered more than 100 discussions and training about software development and entrepreneurship. Lately, he's been actively talking about Microsoft Windows Azure and iOS app development, and also delivering regular iOS app development training.

He's majoring in Physics from the famous Institute of Technology, Bandung (ITB), yet, he's been spending more than half of his life in the IT field. He lives in Bandung, Indonesia, with his two dogs, Cocoa and Kinect, and hopefully, will soon be joined by his soon-to-be wife, Gina.

I dedicate this book to the knowledge seekers, the ones who always stay hungry and foolish.

With this book, I commemorate the late Steve Jobs for always being my role model and an endless inspiration. Thanks to Steve and Apple for the iCloud, without which I have nothing to write about.

Thanks to my fellow DyCoders (Helmi and others) who kept working on my job while I was working on this book. Thanks to the fellow communities for always sharing their knowledge, and fellow professionals for challenging me. Also, thanks to my fellow author, Fauzan, without whom I would have accomplished only a few chapters within the given time. And thanks to the Packt Publishing team without whom this book would never have been published.

Special thanks to my dynamic duo, Cocoa and Kinect, who are named after the best app development framework and 3D motion sensor in the world, for keeping me company night after night. Though they will probably never read it since they are too busy with their bone, plus they are dogs.

I also thank my parents enormously for their unconditional love and everything else and for making me who I am now. Mere words are not enough to thank them, but I've tried anyway.

Lastly, I'd like to thank my soon-to-be wife, Gina Rizka Ariany, who is a rare combination of brains, beauty, and humor, for always believing in me, for relentlessly giving me thrust and lift force, and for everything else in the years to come. And thanks for the coffee I always miss.

Fauzan Alfi lives in Bandung, Jawa Barat, Indonesia, with his family. At the time of writing this book, he was still a student majoring in Architecture from the Institute of Technology, Bandung (ITB). He has been using Mac ever since 2007. Admiring how well-designed and sophisticated Apple technology is, he joined MakeMac, a well-known Apple website with news and guides to using Apple products in Indonesia, as a writer and has been writing for 5 years.

He also supports the Open Web movement and joined Mozilla as a volunteer and representative. He's also a blogger and contributes to many communities in his hometown. You can contact him by visiting his blog on www.fauzanalfi.com or mention him on Twitter @fauzanalfi.

First of all, thanks to God Almighty for guiding me always. I'd like to thank my parents, Agus and Siti Rakhmawati, for supporting me during all days and nights of my book writing period. Thanks to my fellow co-author, Andri for this amazing opportunity. Thanks to Packt Publishing for supporting us from beginning until this book is published. Thanks to my brother, Salman, all my fellow friends at Ikatan Mahasiswa Arsitektur Gunadharma Institut Teknologi Bandung and all my friends from fellow communities in Bandung for the support I got. One last thing. Thanks Steve for inspiring us.

About the Reviewers

Daniel Mühlbachler became interested in Computer Science shortly after starting high school, where he was later developing web applications as part of the scholarship program for outstanding pupils.

Besides having a profound knowledge of web development, such as PHP, HTML, and CSS, he has also worked with a variety of other programming languages, such as Java, Groovy/Grails, Objective-C, MATLAB, and C, and is skilled in Linux server administration. For his Bachelor's thesis at Johannes Kepler University in Linz, Austria, he worked on aerosol satellite data processing for mobile visualization, where he also got familiar with MongoDB and processing big amounts of data.

He enjoys solving challenging problems and is always keen to work with new technologies, especially with Big Data, functional programming, optimization, and NoSQL database-related ones.

More detailed information about his experience and contact details can be found at `www.muehlbachler.org` and `www.linkedin.com/in/danielmuehlbachler`.

Sergio Martínez-Losa Del Rincón lives in Spain. He is a software engineer and a serial entrepreneur. He has always liked to write technical documents as well as programming in several languages. Nowadays, he focuses all his efforts on game development and mobile technologies such as iPhone or Android. He likes cloud technologies, especially iCloud, because it presents a new way to explore and share your data; he also likes web development with .NET and Java.

In 2012, with the help of two other friends, he started an indie game studio called DoubleEqual (`http://www.doubleequal.com`), where they had a little success with some of their games. He always looks forward to learn about new technologies; he likes app development for iOS and Android as well as games with cocos2d-x and SDL.

www.PacktPub.com

Support files, eBooks, discount offers, and more

You might want to visit www.PacktPub.com for support files and downloads related to your book.

Did you know that Packt offers eBook versions of every book published, with PDF and ePub files available? You can upgrade to the eBook version at www.PacktPub.com and as a print book customer, you are entitled to a discount on the eBook copy. Get in touch with us at service@packtpub.com for more details.

At www.PacktPub.com, you can also read a collection of free technical articles, sign up for a range of free newsletters and receive exclusive discounts and offers on Packt books and eBooks.

http://PacktLib.PacktPub.com

Do you need instant solutions to your IT questions? PacktLib is Packt's online digital book library. Here, you can access, read and search across Packt's entire library of books.

Why Subscribe?

- Fully searchable across every book published by Packt
- Copy and paste, print, and bookmark content
- On demand and accessible via web browser

Free Access for Packt account holders

If you have an account with Packt at www.PacktPub.com, you can use this to access PacktLib today and view nine entirely free books. Simply use your login credentials for immediate access.

Table of Contents

Preface

Ten years ago, we thought **Personal Computer** (**PC**) was the hub of our digital content, where all of our music, photos, and videos are stored and synced across all digital devices. Now, it is the cloud that has become the digital hub. It can be a combination of storage and services stored and run somewhere on the Internet, hence the term cloud computing.

The term "cloud computing" actually has been around since the early days of computers, in which a computation is performed using large-scale mainframes and the clients are only "dumb terminals". But only in 2006, this term seemed more popular than ever when the two software giants, Amazon and Microsoft, introduced their cloud computing platform, soon followed by various cloud computing and storage services, such as Dropbox.

Apple came quite late into the game with its own cloud computing service: the iCloud. However, iCloud is nothing like similar cloud computing services. It hides the complexity so that the users don't need any significant efforts to activate, set up, and use it. It's the technology that indeed works.

Sometimes, it's easy to get lost in that sophisticated world, no matter how simple the iCloud is made by Apple. That is where this book comes to the rescue. This book will walk you through from the moment you turn on your device, activate iCloud, set it up, and start to use it in everyday life.

What this book covers

Chapter 1, Hello, iCloud!, explains what iCloud is and how it works, what features iCloud provides to the users and their devices, and what makes iCloud different from other services.

Chapter 2, Getting Started with iCloud, explains how to get started with iCloud on devices, including a Mac computer, iPhone, iPod touch, iPad, and Windows PC.

Chapter 3, Working with Mail, Contacts, and Calendar, explains how to use Mail, Contacts, and Calendar with iCloud and how to manage the contents across your devices.

Chapter 4, Collaborate with iMessage, Notes, and Reminders, explains how to set up iMessage on devices, use Notes and Reminders, and how to manage the content across your devices.

Chapter 5, Using iPhoto and iTunes with iCloud, explains how to use iCloud with iTunes and iPhoto, access purchased music and movies from your Mac, PC, iOS Device, or Apple TV, and how to set up and use iTunes Match across your devices.

Chapter 6, Syncing Your Contents with iCloud, explains how to store and manage various types of content in the cloud, including documents, apps, bookmarks, and iBooks data.

Chapter 7, Exploring iCloud Apps, explains how to use the `icloud.com` web portal, as well as certain iCloud apps, such as Find my iPhone, Find my Friends, and iWork.

Chapter 8, Backing Up Devices to iCloud, explains how iCloud backs up your iOS device, how to back up and restore an iPhone, iPad, or iPod touch using iCloud, and the various storage options available on iCloud.

Chapter 9, Using iCloud with OS X, explains how to use certain Mac-specific iCloud features using Mac OS X, including iCloud-enabled apps, and Back to my Mac.

Chapter 10, Using iCloud with Windows, explains certain Windows-specific aspects of iCloud, such as using the iCloud Control Panel, and setting up iCloud with Microsoft Outlook.

What you need for this book

For this book, you will need the following hardware and software:

- A Mac computer running OS X Lion (v10.7.5) or later. OS X Mavericks (v10.9) is recommended.

- A PC running Microsoft Windows Vista (SP2), 7, 8, or later. Windows 7 or later is recommended.

- iOS devices, including iPhone, iPad, iPad mini, and iPod touch, running iOS 6 or later.

- iTunes 10.5 or later installed on a Mac or PC. iTunes 11 or later is recommended.

- Microsoft Office Outlook 2007 or later installed on a PC running Windows.

The latest version of each software is recommended in order to make the most out of iCloud. Other types of software required in this book is downloadable from the Internet with the step-by-step instructions given in the relevant chapters.

Who this book is for

This book is aimed towards all users who want to know more about iCloud and use it in the best way for your daily productivity. Any knowledge of cloud computing or programming is not required at all.

You will need to know how to browse the Web using any modern web browsers, understand how to use productivity tools such as e-mail, contacts directory, and online calendar, and also be familiar with using a computer and/or iOS devices.

Conventions

In this book, you will find a number of styles of text that distinguish between different kinds of information. Here are some examples of these styles, and an explanation of their meaning.

Code words in folder names, filenames, file extensions, pathnames, dummy URLs, user input, and Twitter handles are shown as follows: "If you have an `@me.com` e-mail address even if you aren't subscribed to MobileMe, Apple will be reactivated for e-mail when you're signing up for iCloud."

New terms and important words are shown in bold. Words that you see on the screen, in menus or dialog boxes for example, appear in the text like this: "clicking on the **Next** button moves you to the next screen."

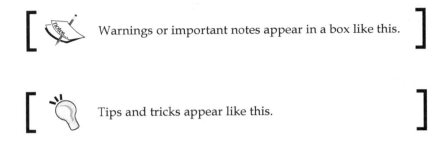

> Warnings or important notes appear in a box like this.

> Tips and tricks appear like this.

Reader feedback

Feedback from our readers is always welcome. Let us know what you think about this book—what you liked or may have disliked. Reader feedback is important for us to develop titles that you really get the most out of.

To send us general feedback, simply send an e-mail to feedback@packtpub.com, and mention the book title through the subject of your message.

If there is a topic that you have expertise in and you are interested in either writing or contributing to a book, see our author guide on www.packtpub.com/authors.

Customer support

Now that you are the proud owner of a Packt book, we have a number of things to help you to get the most from your purchase.

Errata

Although we have taken every care to ensure the accuracy of our content, mistakes do happen. If you find a mistake in one of our books—maybe a mistake in the text or the code—we would be grateful if you would report this to us. By doing so, you can save other readers from frustration and help us improve subsequent versions of this book. If you find any errata, please report them by visiting http://www.packtpub.com/support, selecting your book, clicking on the **errata submission form** link, and entering the details of your errata. Once your errata are verified, your submission will be accepted and the errata will be uploaded to our website, or added to any list of existing errata, under the Errata section of that title.

Piracy

Piracy of copyright material on the Internet is an ongoing problem across all media. At Packt, we take the protection of our copyright and licenses very seriously. If you come across any illegal copies of our works, in any form, on the Internet, please provide us with the location address or website name immediately so that we can pursue a remedy.

Please contact us at copyright@packtpub.com with a link to the suspected pirated material.

We appreciate your help in protecting our authors, and our ability to bring you valuable content.

Questions

You can contact us at questions@packtpub.com if you are having a problem with any aspect of the book, and we will do our best to address it.

1
Hello, iCloud!

Nowadays, the term *cloud computing* is a hype; it is something that we often refer to as a new revolution. However, we often end up misunderstanding it.

We think of cloud computing as a product of the early 21st century, however cloud computing has actually been around for quite a long time. It can be dated back to the early days of the computer era in the 1960s, wherein the computation was performed by large-scale mainframe and client computers, also called dumb terminal or thin client, having no processing capability. But it was only in 2006 that this term seemed more popular than ever when the two software giants, Amazon and Microsoft, introduced their cloud computing platforms, followed soon by various cloud computing and storage services such as Dropbox.

Cloud computing essentially comprises of performing computations in a large number of connected computers over the Internet. The computations can be as simple as managing and synchronizing content or highly-distributed software operations. What these operations have in common, is the sharing of resources between users and tenants to achieve coherence and economies of scale. It's like sharing electricity. By doing that, the initial investment cost of computing infrastructure can be reduced to none, and the monthly usage cost can be reduced as well. In other words, users don't have to purchase and deploy one or more dedicated servers on the Internet in order to share files. For example, besides sharing the computing resources (processors, memory, or storage), cloud computing can be beneficial by allocating resources on demand. Essentially, you pay for what you use.

During its evolution, cloud computing has come a long way from just sharing computing resources to providing seamless integration and synchronization between devices, both for PC and mobile devices. The latter is where **iCloud** comes into place.

2000s – PC as a digital hub

The personal computer (PC) has evolved throughout the years from the age of productivity in the 1980s, where people used it for spreadsheets and databases, to the age of networking in the 1990s, where it connected to the Internet, and entered into its third age in the early 2000s, the age of digital lifestyle. Consumers had increasingly started using all kinds of digital devices, such as digital cameras, camcorders, music players, and PDAs, but these devices didn't make sense without a computer. The personal computer was going to become the center or digital hub of this new digital lifestyle, making all its pieces — music, photos, movies, contacts and data — come together.

On January 9, 2001, Apple's CEO, Steve Jobs, outlined Apple's "digital hub" strategy. The iMac became the center of a user's digital life, managing content on cameras, video cameras, mobile phones, and media players. It's a plan that put Apple's new OS X at the place where the Internet and the rest of a user's digital life meets. It's worked out well over the past decade; Apple's shares have risen by 2917.9 percent.

Microsoft, with its Windows operating system, went with a similar strategy with the release of Windows XP on October 25, 2001. Windows XP introduced — among other new features — a streamlined multimedia experience dubbed as "Media Center". Media Center emphasizes on DVD playback, TV tuner, DVR functionality, and remote controls. Then, Microsoft also introduced **Microsoft Plus! Digital Media Edition** for Windows XP and as a part of the Microsoft Plus! product line, designed to give users who own standard PCs more features for editing and playing with media files.

The introduction of iCloud in 2011 put an end to the *PC as a digital hub* strategy, especially for Apple.

2010s – cloud is the digital hub

As Apple started the initiative of using PC as the digital hub, it also ended it with the iCloud. And that's not without reason. Every day, mobile devices are coming closer and closer to match PC capabilities. It is time to demote the PC to be just another device on par with mobile devices. Now, cloud is the new digital hub where everything gets stored and synced to it. Add or update calendar items, contacts, notes, e-mails, photos, songs, videos, books, and it's all available in the cloud and immediately synced across devices. iCloud was the first notable initiative of positioning the cloud as the digital hub.

For the sake of history, iCloud is not Apple's first attempt in the cloud computing space. There was **MobileMe** that offered similar synchronization services for an annual subscription fee. MobileMe's primary purpose was to keep certain files synchronized among multiple devices that included e-mails, contacts, calendars, browser bookmarks, photo galleries, and Apple iWeb and iDisk services. The MobileMe service was discontinued entirely on June 30, 2012 and replaced by iCloud.

What is iCloud?

In terms of cloud computing, iCloud is a different type of cloud computing that puts more focus on keeping content synced across endpoint devices such as iOS devices (iPads, iPhones, iPod touches, and Apple TVs), Macs, and Windows computers. It's more about synchronization services rather than infrastructure or platform services in which you move the processing and data from local computers to Internet-based servers and resources.

What can iCloud do for you?

There are lots of things that you can do with iCloud, and iCloud can do so much for you as well. We will cover most of the features in this book; some of them were recently introduced in the Apple's annual developer event, **Worldwide Developer Conference 2013**.

iCloud offers a lot of services that you can work with. There are Mails, Contacts, and Calendar as the main services, iMessage for sending messages or other content, Notes and Reminders, Photo Stream for keeping pictures taken with your devices and sharing them, iTunes in the cloud, iTunes Match, Documents in the Cloud, Backup, Find My iPhone for searching your lost devices, and more. We will look at all the services in the following sections

Mail, Contacts, and Calendar

Mail, Contacts, and Calendar are the three main services in iCloud. These are free to use and available for every single user. For Mail itself, Apple provides 5 GB storage to use, shared with other iCloud services. For more information, you can read *Chapter 3*, *Working with Mail, Contacts, and Calendar*.

iMessage

iMessage was introduced by Apple in 2011, and allows you to send/receive messages, pictures, contacts' information, or even locations from an Apple device to/from another Apple device. iMessage is available on Mac and iOS devices. For more information, you can read *Chapter 4, Collaborate with iMessage, Notes, and Reminders.*

Notes and Reminders

Notes and Reminders are two simple, yet powerful productivity tools. Notes keeps your notes and syncs them all to your Mac and iOS devices. Reminders lets you write some to-do lists and gather them into groups. Just like Notes, it also syncs to all your Mac and iOS devices. For more information, you can read *Chapter 4, Collaborate with iMessage, Notes, and Reminders.*

Photo Stream

Photo Stream is the best feature for those who love taking pictures from their iOS devices. This feature automatically uploads all the pictures taken by you and syncs them all to your Mac, iOS devices, and Apple TV. For more information, you can read *Chapter 5, Using iPhoto and iTunes with iCloud.*

iTunes in the Cloud

After you've bought music, movies, TV shows, or apps from the iTunes Store, iTunes in the Cloud lets you download everything you've bought again. Not just that, when you buy an app or a music album from your iOS device, iTunes downloads the same content you bought at the same time on your Mac. So you don't need to sync your iOS device just for transferring the content. For more information, you can read *Chapter 5, Using iPhoto and iTunes with iCloud.*

iTunes Match

iTunes Match is a subscription service from Apple to put all your iTunes music libraries on iCloud. By activating this feature, you can access and listen to your entire music library wherever you are. iTunes Match not only works for the music you've purchased from the iTunes Store but also the music you've purchased from any of the sources, including music imported from CD. For more information, you can read *Chapter 5, Using iPhoto and iTunes with iCloud.*

Documents in the Cloud

With Documents in the Cloud, you can store documents such as text documents, spreadsheets, and presentations to the cloud. It is different from other services, as it also syncs your documents including all the changes made to them. It's really useful if you work on multiple devices. For more information, you can read *Chapter 6, Syncing Your Contents with iCloud*.

Find My iPhone

Find My iPhone is a service that helps you to locate your iOS devices and Mac computers wherever they are. On Mac, this feature is known as **Find My Mac**. This feature is really useful when you lose your device or it's stolen because you can track it. In iOS 7, Find My iPhone locks your iPhone, so a thief can't use the device or restore it as a new device because it will keep asking for the original Apple ID and password provided when it's first successfully activated. For more information, you can read *Chapter 7, Exploring iCloud Apps*.

iCloud.com

The `iCloud.com` website is the place to see nearly all your stored data on the iCloud server. It also has eight web apps that you can access from any desktop web browser: Mail, Contacts, Calendars, Notes, Reminders, Find My iPhone, and iWork. For more information, you can read *Chapter 7, Exploring iCloud Apps*.

Back to My Mac

With Back to My Mac feature, you can easily and securely access your remote Mac computers from other Mac computers over the Internet. You can easily browse through your files and drag-and-drop them between remote and local Mac computers. You can also do screen sharing in order to control your remote computer as if you were sitting in front of it. For more details, please refer to *Chapter 9, Using iCloud with OS X*.

Back up your devices

iCloud allows you to back up your iOS devices directly to the cloud. You can also restore them directly from iCloud. Since your iOS device directly interacts with iCloud, there's no computer needed to activate and use this feature. For more information, you can read *Chapter 8, Backing Up Devices to iCloud*.

Collaborating with OS X

Since OS X Mountain Lion (10.8) has been released, Apple intensely integrates iCloud with OS X. Stock or built-in apps are already integrated with the iCloud services and many third-party apps. You will learn how they collaborate, and how to use iCloud for productivity. On the next version to be released, OS X Mavericks (10.9), we're going to see deeper iCloud integration into the system. For more information, you can read *Chapter 9, Using iCloud with OS X*.

Collaborating with Microsoft Windows

Not only for OS X, Apple lets you access some iCloud services and integrates them with Windows PC. With **iCloud Control Panel**, which needs to be downloaded and installed separately, you can access Mail, Contacts, and Calendar with Microsoft Outlook 2007 or later. For more information, you can read *Chapter 10, Using iCloud with Windows*.

At the time of writing this book, Apple has announced two new features for iCloud during the Apple Worldwide Developers Conference (WWDC) on June 10, 2013: iWork for iCloud and iCloud Keychain. We will not cover these features in detail here since they are still in the beta stage and may be changed over time until their final release. The next section gives a short explanation about them.

iWork for iCloud

iWork for iCloud is different from the current iWork app on `iCloud.com`. With iWork for iCloud, Apple brings Pages, Numbers, and Keynotes to the Web. So you can create and edit new documents directly from a web browser. You can also import any Microsoft Office documents and edit them directly on iWork for iCloud. This feature is available as a beta version for all iCloud users.

iCloud Keychain

With iCloud Keychain, Apple syncs all of your saved passwords to all of your devices. It also helps you by suggesting a password when you forget it. It stores them securely because they're encrypted with robust 256-bit AES encryption. This feature will be available on OS X Mavericks and iOS 7, as shown in the following screenshot:

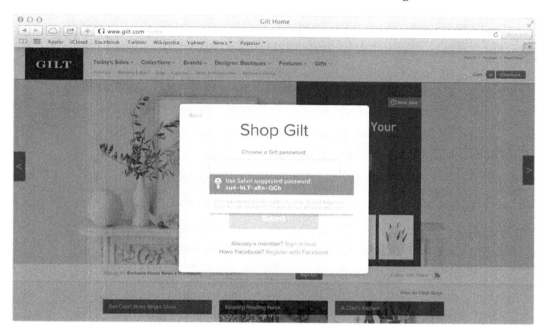

How does iCloud differ from other cloud services?

In terms of cloud computing, iCloud is not commonly understood as cloud computing. Most of the users who use iCloud don't even know that they are using some form of cloud computing and that is okay. Instead, iCloud is the typical offering from Apple; one that's turnkey and user-friendly so that consumers never see most of its underlying complexities. All they know is that their data magically syncs among devices, and they don't care whether it's via cloud computing or carrier pigeons.

Nevertheless, we need to differentiate iCloud from other common cloud computing services.

iCloud versus Windows Azure

While there are some rumors that some parts of iCloud services run on top of Windows Azure, regardless of whether it is true or not, iCloud is different from Windows Azure or its rival Amazon Web Services. Amazon and Azure focus on **Infrastructure as a Service (IaaS)** and **Platform as a Service (PaaS)** that allow application developers and IT professionals to develop and deploy applications or services to some servers on the Internet, instead of doing it with their own servers. It is essentially about moving the processing and data from local (private/ on-premise) computers to Internet-based servers and resources. In contrast, iCloud is about users, which allows user's content to be synchronized all the time between devices, PC (OS X and Windows-based), and iOS devices. For example, iCloud won't allow web developers to host their websites / web applications.

iCloud versus Dropbox

As explained before, iCloud is basically a cloud synchronization service. What about Dropbox or other similar services? Isn't Dropbox about keeping files synchronized between devices as well?

The defining feature of iCloud, when compared to Dropbox, is that the content/files are in a virtual silo per app. iCloud has been designed specifically to be application-centric and deeply integrated into each application that uses it. When you edit a document using Pages on your Mac, it will be synced to Pages on your iPhone or iPad. This Pages document is only available in the Pages app on each device. Your Keynote presentations are only available in the Keynote app on each device and not accessible by the Pages app on iOS devices. So are the photos shared using the Photo Stream feature; they are only available in the Photo Stream app in iOS devices and iPhoto on Mac.

Dropbox is different; it is basically a folder on your hard drive that syncs to a virtual folder, then in turn syncs to another folder on another device you have and set. Basically, it is a large folder in the cloud that apps can tie in to, and you can have it on most of your devices and computers. It is the most flexible and least inventive, while iCloud is the most inventive and least flexible.

Summary

iCloud is a part of the vision that Apple's late CEO, Steve Jobs had to use the cloud as the digital hub instead of computers. Unlike other cloud services, iCloud offers a seamless experience within all Apple devices you own. It's a different type of cloud computing where it's more focused on your contents and syncs them across all devices. iCloud offers a bunch of services you can use, which range from Mail to Reminders, storing your pictures with Photo Stream and documents with Documents in the Cloud, backing up your iOS devices, and locating your mobile devices with Find My iPhone. In the next chapter, you'll learn more on how to set up all these services and use them on your devices.

2
Getting Started with iCloud

Now, you know what iCloud is and how important it is to use with your Mac, iOS devices (iPhone, iPad, and iPod touch), or even for your Windows PC. It's time for you to get started with iCloud.

In this chapter, you will learn step-by-step how to sign up for an iCloud account on your devices and how to manage it easily. For those who already have a MobileMe account, you need to migrate it first to iCloud. Before we get started, we need to understand what an Apple ID is and how it's related to iCloud (or even with all Apple services).

About Apple ID

If you've bought or downloaded anything, whether it's music from the iTunes Store or apps from the App Store, it implies that you already have an Apple ID. If you have used OS X for a long time, you should have an Apple ID, since Apple prompted you to have one when you booted your Mac for the first time.

So then, what is an Apple ID? It's an account created for you to use all services that Apple provides. It's easy to get one and it's free! However, sometimes you do not realize that you've already had one. Apple ID is used not only in their stores but also for the Apple Developer Program, Discussion Forum, Game Center, and Facetime.

Mostly, Apple IDs are easily recognized if an e-mail address ends with @mac.com, or @me.com, or @icloud.com as username for its account. These addresses are coming from Apple services (@mac.com from .Mac and @me.com from MobileMe). It's okay if you're using some other e-mail address as your Apple ID username. But if you want to use iCloud, you need to create a new e-mail address that ends with @icloud.com.

Everyone is allowed to have more than one Apple ID, but I recommend you to have only one account as a primary one that will be used for iCloud. It's not possible to merge multiple accounts into a single Apple ID account. If you want to check your Apple ID account or change the password, go to `appleid.apple.com`, as shown in the following screenshot:

Signing up for iCloud

It's really easy to sign up for an iCloud account. All you have to own is an Apple device. Why? Unlike any other services, you cannot sign up for iCloud directly from its website. You must sign up directly from any Apple device, including Mac, iOS devices (except Apple TV), and Windows PC.

System requirements

Before we go through to sign up process, make sure that your devices meet some recommended system requirements.

iOS devices

To use iCloud with proper experience, your iOS devices should meet following system requirements:

- **iOS version**: iOS 5 or later. Availability of iCloud features depends on the iOS version.
- **Devices**:
    - ○ iPhone 3GS or later
    - ○ iPad 2 or later (including iPad mini)
    - ○ iPod touch third generation or later

Mac

To use iCloud with proper experience, your Mac computer should meet following system requirements:

- OS X Lion 10.7.5 or later
- iTunes 11 or later (for iTunes in the Cloud and iTunes Match)
- iPhoto 11 version 9.4 or later, or Aperture 3.4 or later (for Photo Stream)
- Safari 6 or later to access iCloud, Bookmarks, and iCloud Tabs sync

Windows PC

To use iCloud with proper experience, your PC or the Boot Camp installation should meet following system requirements:

- Microsoft Windows 7 or later
- iCloud Control Panel 2.1 or later
- iTunes 11 or later (for iTunes in the Cloud and iTunes Match)
- Outlook 2007 or later (for Mail, Contacts, and Calendar)
- Safari 5.1.7 or later, Internet Explorer 9 or later (for iCloud.com and Bookmarks sync), Firefox 16 or later, or Chrome 23 or later

Mac

For Mac users, you need to authenticate your Mac with Apple ID to use iCloud services. There are some steps you must go through and they might be different depending on your Mac, whether it's a fresh-from-the-box Mac or an existing Mac.

For new Mac

When you boot a new Mac for the first time, you will see a welcome screen and OS X will guide you to set up your Mac for the first time. It will also guide you to create your first Apple ID that you need in order to use iCloud services and other Apple services. Follow the onscreen instructions to complete the process until you see OS X desktop and the infamous finder.

For existing Mac

To get iCloud built right on your Mac, make sure that your Mac is running OS X Lion 10.7.5 or later. On that update, it will show the iCloud preference pane on the **System Preferences** page. It's better to upgrade your Mac to OS X Mountain Lion to get the most out of every iCloud feature. To set up iCloud on your Mac, perform the following steps:

1. Go to the Apple menu on the top-left corner of the screen.

2. Choose **System Preferences**. You can see **iCloud** on Internet and services. Click on the **iCloud** tab, as shown in the following screenshot:.

3. If you already have an Apple ID, enter your Apple ID and your password.

4. If you don't have one, click on **Create an Apple ID** and follow the onscreen instructions.

Windows PC

In the MobileMe era, Apple has provided an application called MobileMe Control Panel to configure MobileMe services and collaborated with Windows services, including Windows Explorer (or File Explorer on Windows 8).

Similar to MobileMe, iCloud Control Panel is available to all iCloud users who use Windows PC or have Windows installed on their Mac. For more information, you can refer to the *Configuring iCloud Control Panel* section in *Chapter 10, Using iCloud with Windows*.

To set iCloud on Windows OS, perform the following steps:

1. Install the iCloud Control Panel on Windows.

2. Once it's installed, launch iCloud Control Panel.

3. Enter your Apple ID as your iCloud account and your password. If you don't have one, you should create and activate it first from any Apple device.

 To download iCloud Control Panel for Windows, go to http://www.icloud.com/icloudcontrolpanel.

iOS device

Just like Mac users, you need to authenticate your iOS device with Apple ID to use iCloud services. There are some steps you must go through and they might be different depending on whether your iOS device is a new or existing one.

For new iOS devices

Since Apple released iOS 5, you will see a similar welcome screen on any new iOS device to guide the new user to get started with their devices, including Apple ID and iCloud setup for entire services. The following steps will help you to go thorough the welcome screen of iOS:

1. Turn on your new iOS device by simply pressing and holding the sleep button on the top right of the device.

2. Your device will show you the welcome screen. Follow the instructions until the **Set Up iPhone** or **Set Up iPod touch** screen is shown.

3. Choose **Set Up as New iPhone** for your iPhone (same for iPod touch or iPad), and then click on the **Next** button. If you want to restore your new iOS device using iCloud Backup, you can refer to *Chapter 8, Backing Up Devices to iCloud*.

4. Now, you will see the Apple ID screen. To sign up for an iCloud account, you must have an Apple ID. Click on the **Create a free Apple ID** button to create one.

5. Enter your birthday date. Then click on **Next**.

6. Choose **Get a free iCloud email address** and then click on **Next**.

7. Enter a username that you want to have as your iCloud account and also for your iCloud Mail. You can't change your username after your account is created, or else you'll have to create another iCloud account with a different username. Then click on **Next**.

8. Your iOS device will show you terms and conditions for iOS, iCloud, and Game Center. Click on **Agree** to continue the process.

9. The **Set Up iCloud** screen will appear. Choose **Use iCloud** to activate iCloud services on your iOS devices. Then click on **Next**.

10. If you want to use iCloud to back up your iOS device daily, choose **Back Up to iCloud**. If not, you can choose **Back Up to My Computer**.

11. One of the coolest services on iCloud is the Find My iPhone app. Choose **Use Find My iPhone** (or iPod touch/iPad) to activate it. To know more about Find My iPhone, you can refer to *Chapter 7, Exploring iCloud Apps*.

12. Continue following the rest of the instructions until you can start using your iOS device.

For existing iOS devices

iCloud is built right in iOS, starting from iOS 5 in October 2011. To get the most of all iCloud features, I recommend you to upgrade your device to the latest version of iOS. You're able to choose which iCloud apps or services you want to activate on the current device. You may activate only apps or services you want and it is possible to have different settings between one device and another. To activate iCloud for an existing iOS device, perform the following steps:

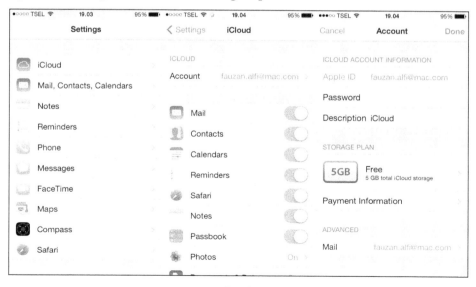

1. On your homescreen, tap **Settings** and choose **iCloud**.

2. Enter your Apple ID and your password, if you have one. Follow any onscreen instructions.

3. Once you see the list of iCloud apps (Mail, Contacts, and so on), with the ON/OFF toggles on the right-hand side, you can choose which apps you want to activate on your current device and which you do not.

4. If you don't have an Apple ID, tap the **Get Free Apple ID** button at the bottom of the screen. Follow any onscreen instruction to create your Apple ID and activate iCloud on your current device.

Migrating from MobileMe

If you are a MobileMe subscriber and would like to use your current @mac.com or @me.com as your Apple ID for iCloud, you can migrate it by entering your @mac.com or @me.com e-mail address while setting up iCloud on your device. Your MobileMe account will then be migrated to iCloud.

If you have an @me.com e-mail address, even if you aren't subscribed to MobileMe, your Apple account will be reactivated for e-mail when you're signing up for iCloud. But, if you had an @mac.com e-mail address that you got from .Mac, unfortunately, you can't use it anymore, so you must then set up a new @icloud.com e-mail address that you can use for iCloud.

It's important to have a verified e-mail address associated with your Apple ID to set up iCloud. To add one, go to appleid.apple.com, sign in with your @me.com or @mac.com e-mail address, then add a valid e-mail address to your account.

Once your MobileMe account is migrated to iCloud, you will get a welcome message just like other new iCloud users.

Before the end of September 2013, every MobileMe subscriber will be given 20 GB extra storage on iCloud. After that, the storage will be automatically reduced to 5 GB free storage. Like the rest of the iCloud subscribers, migrated MobileMe subscribers can get more storage by paying an annual storage subscription. To learn more about this, please refer to *Chapter 8, Backing Up Devices to iCloud*.

 To get more information on MobileMe migration to iCloud, Apple has provided a support page: `http://support.apple.com/kb/HT4436`.

Managing your iCloud account

Managing your iCloud account is easy because you can access it from any device you have. You can use your Mac, Windows PC, iOS devices, or browser in any computer to know your account status and configuration by visiting `www.icloud.com`. To manage more, you can open the iCloud preference pane on your Mac or iCloud Control Panel on your Windows PC, as shown in the following screenshot:

On the iCloud preference pane, you'll see a list of iCloud services that are available for your Mac. Check on the box to activate each service that you want. More detail on each service will be included in later chapters of this book. You can also check your current iCloud storage capacity and how many GB are available on your account, as shown in the following screenshot:

Click on the **Manage** button to see all applications in both Mac and iOS that have stored some data on iCloud and iOS device backups. You can delete the data by simply selecting an app and data or document you want to delete, and click on the **Delete** button. If you want to delete all of the documents and data for a selected app, click on **Delete All**.

To configure iCloud on your iOS device, simply go to **Settings | iCloud** and you'll see a panel similar to that in Mac. If you are a Windows PC user, you will learn more about iCloud Control Panel and iCloud integration to Windows-specific applications in *Chapter 10, Using iCloud with Windows*.

Summary

In order to use most Apple services, including iCloud, every Apple products user must create an Apple ID. If you buy a new Apple device with the latest version of iOS or OS X, it will prompt you to sign in to iCloud with your existing Apple ID or create one. If you already have any Apple devices, make sure they have the latest version of the operating system and supports iCloud.

For Windows PC users, check if your PC meets the requirements and then install iCloud Control Panel. You can't create a new Apple ID or iCloud account on Control Panel. You must create it on an Apple device, whether it's a Mac or an iOS device (iPhone, iPad, and iPod touch).

3
Working with Mail, Contacts, and Calendar

In the previous chapter, you learned how to set up iCloud on Mac, Windows PC, and iOS devices. Basically, there are three main services in iCloud: Mail, Contacts, and Calendar. Everyone who has signed up for iCloud is given these services by default. Now, we will look at how to work with Mail, Contacts, and Calendar for your daily tasks and how they will synchronize between your devices automatically. Just like *Steve Jobs* said, *"It just works."*

Mail

Every iCloud account is associated with a single iCloud e-mail address. Generally, the e-mail address you get ends with `@me.com` or `@icloud.com` for new users. This e-mail address also acts as your Apple ID.

You can access your iCloud e-mail address on the Web or from a specific application on your Mac or Windows PC. On Mac, you can access it using the **Mail** app, and on Windows PC, you need to install Microsoft Outlook 2007 or later to access it (see the *iCloud and Microsoft Outlook* section in *Chapter 10, Using iCloud with Windows*).

Setting up mail on your iOS device

To start using **Mail** on your iOS device, you need to enable it first in the iCloud settings. Make sure that you have set the **Mail** toggle to the green position, as shown in the following screenshot. There's no extra step to enable an iCloud e-mail address.

Now you can access your iCloud e-mail address on the **Mail** app. When you configure multiple e-mail accounts, you should see the iCloud logo on **Accounts** and the iCloud label on **Inboxes**. If you configure the iCloud e-mail address only, you should be directed to the iCloud e-mail folders screen:

Tap the **iCloud** label in **Inboxes** and you can view all of your messages. You can change the name for your iCloud e-mail account instead of using the default name, **iCloud**. To see all iCloud e-mail folders, tap **iCloud** on **Accounts** and you can see all folders including **Drafts**, **Sent Items**, and **Junk**.

Adding more than one iCloud e-mail account on iOS

If you have more than one iCloud account, you can add it to your iOS device by simply going to **Settings | Mail, Contacts, Calendars | Add Account... | iCloud**. Enter your iCloud account information and set the **Mail** toggle to the ON position.

Configuring mail settings on iOS devices

Since iOS 6, you can configure your e-mail settings to the next level just like on a desktop. You can configure how the **Mail** app fetches your messages, change your signatures, and so on. You can find out everything about Mail configuration on the **Mail, Contacts, Calendars** screen in the **Settings** app. Now, we'll explain them all one by one.

iCloud-specific configuration

On the **Settings** app, navigate to **Mail, Contacts, Calendars | iCloud | Account | Advanced | Mail**. There are several settings specific to the iCloud e-mail account you've set up before.

To change a default address that is used when sending messages from your iCloud e-mail account, tap **Email** and choose the address that you want to use by default. You can choose between the @me.com address or the @icloud.com address (or the @mac.com address if you are a .Mac subscriber). You can set which addresses you would like to use when sending messages from your iCloud account. Set the toggle to the green position for the address you used.

iOS also enables you to set your iCloud mailbox behaviors by tapping **Advanced**. In the **Mailbox Behaviors** section, you are allowed to set which folder you want to assign as **Drafts Mailbox**, **Sent Mailbox**, **Deleted Mailbox**, and **Archive Mailbox**. By default, they are assigned to drafts, sent messages, deleted messages, and archive. You are also allowed to choose which mailbox any discarded messages move into. You can choose between **Deleted Mailbox** and **Archive Mailbox**.

You can also configure when your iCloud deleted message will be removed, whether it's after one day, one week, one month, or never.

 Some iCloud specific configurations also appear on other e-mail providers such as Gmail or Yahoo Mail.

Global mail configuration

Besides iCloud-specific configuration, iOS also lets you to set global mail configuration such as quote levels and signatures. These configurations will affect all mail accounts you've set up including iCloud Mail.

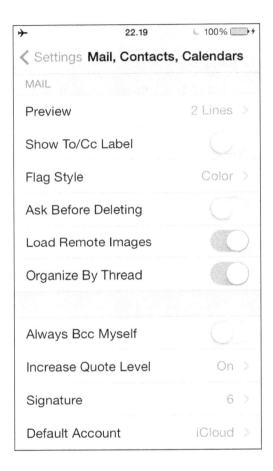

On the **Settings** app, go to **Mail, Contacts, Calendars | iCloud** and you will see the **Mail** section. Let's go through to all the options listed:

- **Preview**: It will set how many lines of the e-mail will be previewed on the folder or Inbox screen.
- **Show To/Cc label**: It can be used to show the **To** and **Cc** labels.

- **Flag Style**: It is used to choose what icon—either **Color** or **Shape**—will be shown when you flag an e-mail and any flagged e-mails.

- **Ask Before Deleting**: It will ask you before deleting any e-mails and prevent you from accidentally deleting anything.

- **Load Remote Images**: It is used to set whether you want to load images on your messages or not.

- **Organize By Thread**: The **Mail** app will organize all conversation e-mails into threads. Threads let you see all mail with the same subject in a series of conversations so that you can track them easily.

- **Always Bcc Myself**: You can toggle it green to add your e-mail address on the **Bcc** field automatically.

- **Increase Quote Level**: Use this option to add a level of indentation when you forward or reply to an e-mail.

- **Signature**: You can add a signature at the end of your e-mail. You can assign the same signature for all accounts or different signatures for each account.

- **Default account**: You can assign which e-mail account you want to use as the default account for the entire OS, especially when sending a message outside of the **Mail** app.

Fetch or push your message to iOS device

Most e-mail providers allow users to push a new message soon after it comes to their account. Apple itself provides push mail capability to all iCloud e-mail accounts. So, every new piece of data will be pushed to your iOS devices directly from the server.

If you don't want to get a new message every time it arrives, the **Mail** app can fetch it manually and you can set a schedule for it. It can be every 15 minutes, 30 minutes, hourly, or the **Mail** app will fetch new messages manually when you open the app. The schedule is only used when you toggle the **Push** option to OFF, or for providers, which do not support push e-mail. If you want to save your battery power, it's better to fetch new data less frequently.

Notify new mail on iOS Notification Center

Since iOS 5, Apple introduced **Notification Center**, where every push notifications for your iOS device are gathered. Also, you can configure if you want to be notified for new messages in your e-mail accounts, including iCloud e-mail, and how the device is to notify you.

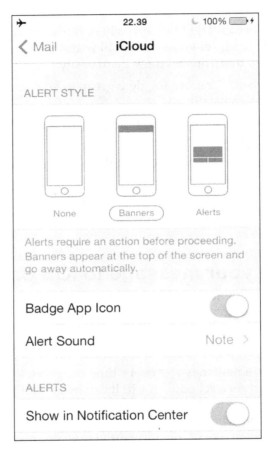

Basically, iOS lets you to choose the alert style for notifications. As shown in the preceding screenshot, there are **Banners** and **Alerts**. **Banners** will appear at the top of the screen and seconds later, it will go away automatically. **Alerts** will show the notification in the middle of the screen and requires the user to take some action before proceeding.

You can change the sound when you receive a new mail as well, using ringtones you've synced to the device. You can also configure whether iOS will show a preview of the new incoming message in alerts, banners, or alerts on the lock screen.

Setting up mail on your Mac

Similar to iOS, you must enable **Mail** on the iCloud preference pane inside your Mac. Make sure that you have checked on the **Mail & Notes** checkbox to activate the service on your Mac, or checked the **Mail** checkbox on the **Internet Accounts** preference pane as shown in the following screenshot. Then, it will automatically configure your iCloud e-mail address to the **Mail** app, Mac OS X's default e-mail application:

> **Adding more than one iCloud e-mail account on Mac**
>
> If you have more than one iCloud account, you're able to add it on your Mac by simply going to **System Preferences | Mail, Contacts & Calendars | iCloud**. Enter your iCloud account information and click on **Sign in**. Follow the instructions and check on the **Mail & Notes** checkbox.

Configuring iCloud mail settings on Mac

To configure your iCloud e-mail on Mac, open the **Mail** app and go to **Mail |
Preferences**. You will see three tabs from iCloud in Accounts: **Accounts Information**,
Mailbox Behaviors, and **Advanced**. Let's find out more.

Accounts information

In this tab, you will see basic information from your iCloud e-mail address. You can
change the description of the account and also choose which alias you want to use
when sending a message with iCloud. To know more on how to create an alias for an
iCloud e-mail address, see the *Working with Mail on iCloud.com* section in this chapter.

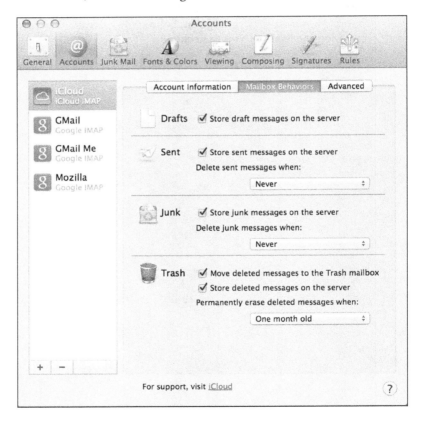

Mailbox behaviors

As shown in the preceding screenshot, you can set mailbox behaviors for each account including the iCloud account. There are **Drafts**, **Sent**, **Junk**, and **Trash**. Let's explore each of them, listed as follows:

- **Drafts**: This is used to store draft messages from your Mac to the iCloud server; make sure you check the checkbox.

- **Sent**: This is used to store all sent messages from your Mac to the iCloud server; make sure you check the checkbox. You can also delete sent messages automatically by time or when quitting **Mail**.

- **Junk**: To store all junk messages from your Mac to the iCloud server, make sure you check the checkbox. You can also delete junk messages automatically by time or when quitting **Mail**.

- **Trash**: You can activate it to move deleted messages to the **Trash** mailbox and store them to the iCloud server or not. You can also permanently erase deleted messages by time or when quitting **Mail**.

Advanced

The **Advanced** option includes:

- If you want **Mail** to check new messages on an iCloud account automatically, check **Include when automatically checking for new messages**.

- There are some options to decide how you manage your messages and their attachments. If you want to keep them all, choose **All messages and their attachments**. If you want to keep all messages only, choose **All messages, but omit attachments**. There are also two other options: **Only messages I've read** and **Don't keep copies of any messages**. It depends on how you want to interact with your messages.

Notify new mail on OS X Notification Center

If you have upgraded your OS X to Mountain Lion or Maverick, you should have the **Notification Center** on your Mac. It's similar to the one in iOS. You can also configure how **Mail** notifies you when you receive a new message. Just open **System Preferences | Notification**. Choose **Mail** and you can choose an alert style that are **Banners** and **Alerts,** as shown in the following screenshot. You also can decide how many recent notifications you want to keep in **Notification Center, Badge app icon** (showing how many unread messages), and choose the sound played when your Mac is receiving notifications:

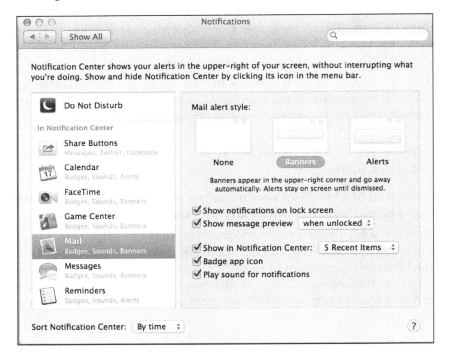

Working with mail on iCloud.com

Apart from native apps, you can also access your iCloud e-mail address directly from the Web. What you need to do is open any supported web browser, such as Safari or Firefox, then go to `iCloud.com`. Enter your iCloud account credentials, which are your Apple ID and password to log in. Then choose **Mail**, as shown in the following screenshot:

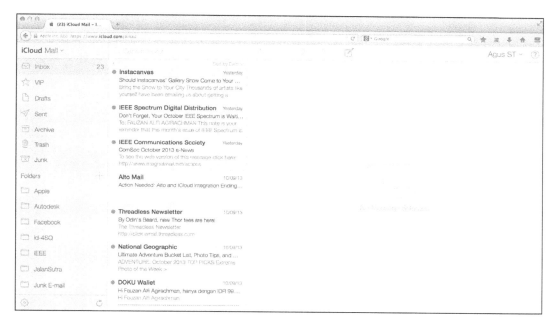

You will see a similar Mail interface like that on the iOS, as shown in the preceding screenshot. On the left pane, you will get your mailbox and folders list. Then in the middle pane, you will see all your messages inside the selected folder and you can read the entire message on the right pane. Also, there are five main buttons on right pane, which are **Reply**, **Flag**, **Trash**, **Move to Folder**, and **Compose**.

Mail aliases on iCloud e-mail

One of advantages you get from iCloud e-mail is mail alias. If you're not familiar with it, mail alias is a feature that lets you create new a e-mail address that points to your iCloud e-mail address but hides the real one. So, the recipients don't know what your real iCloud e-mail address is. It's really useful if you want to share your iCloud e-mail address with the public safely, and prevents you from any unwanted messages. iCloud lets you create up to three e-mail aliases.

To create a mail alias, click on the gear button at the bottom-left corner and choose **Preferences**. Choose **Accounts** and click on the **Add an alias** tab, and it will open a new window. Enter the new e-mail address that you want to be used as your mail alias. It must be different from the real one you own. You can also give it a text label and color label to make it easier for you to sort it out later.

Organize incoming messages with rules

In iCloud Mail , you can organize all new messages, sort them out to any folder, or forward them to any e-mail address automatically by creating rules. Rules help you keep all incoming messages automatically organized into folders.

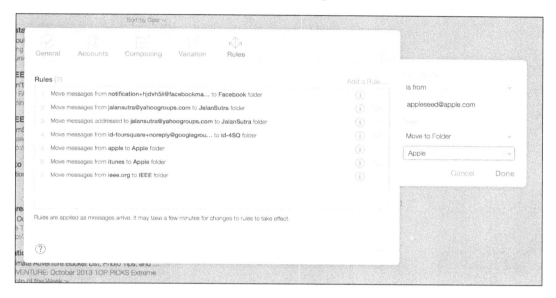

To add a rule, click on the gear button and choose **Rules**. Click on the **Add a Rule** button. A pop-up menu will appear (as shown in the preceding screenshot). Then, decide which messages you want to include in a rule, where they are coming from, and where all those messages will be moved to or forwarded to. It's that simple.

Auto response mail on vacation

If you're on a vacation, iCloud lets you send an auto-response mail to set a reply to any incoming message automatically. So, they will get notified without you opening iCloud e-mail.

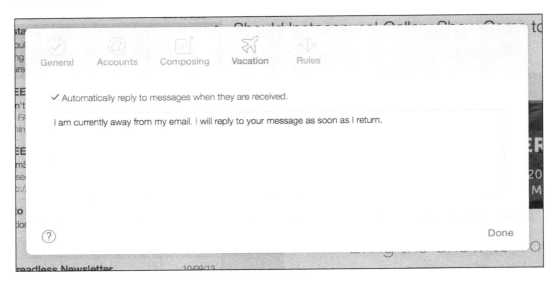

To set it up, click on the gear button and go to **Preferences | Vacation**. Check the **Automatically reply to messages when they are received** checkbox to activate this feature. Then, compose the message you want to send as auto-response mail on textbox.

Contacts

iCloud provides a contacts manager to let you add, edit, and manage contacts on your devices. It does not only manage phone numbers and addresses, but also Twitter handles, Facebook usernames, and even LinkedIn URLs of your contacts. What makes iCloud really special is that it will automatically synchronize them to all your Mac, Windows PC, and iOS devices. That means you will get the same contacts, information available to all your devices that are associated with your iCloud account.

Make sure you've set the **Contacts** toggle to the green position in the iCloud preference panes on your Mac, or iCloud settings on your iOS devices to get iCloud sync works.

Add, edit, and search contacts

In this section, you will learn how to add, edit, and search contacts on a the Mac computer and iOS devices. Essentially, the steps that you will perform on Mac are similar to what you performed on iOS, since both the **Contacts** apps have a similar user interface. So, you won't find any difficulties when you switch from Mac to iOS, or the reverse.

On your iOS devices

To view all iCloud contacts on your iOS devices, open the **Contacts** app or the **Phone** app on iPhone. The app will look like what is shown the following screenshot. To see the contacts groups list, click on the **Groups** button on top-left corner of the screen:

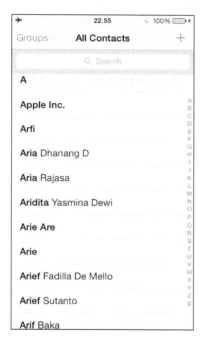

To add a new contact, click on the **+** button on top-right corner of the screen. Then, fill in all the information you want to add on the right pane. On iOS, you can also pick a specific ringtone, text tone, and vibration for your contact, which will be used when he/she is calling or sending an SMS/iMessage to you. You also can add more information by clicking on the **Add Field** button and pick the kind of information you want to add. Click on the **Done** button when you've finished.

On your Mac

To view all iCloud contacts on your Mac, open the **Contacts** app. You will see a user interface that looks like a contact book. On the left pane, you will see the iCloud contacts list and groups list, and the right pane shows the details of the contact that you've selected.

To add a new contact, click on the **+** button on bottom-left corner of the app. Then, fill in all of the information you want to add on the right pane. Click on the **Done** button if you've finished.

Managing contacts with groups

Both Mac OS X and iOS are supporting groups on **Contacts**. This app helps you to gather contacts based on the specific criteria that you want. To create a new contact group, you must do that on your Mac or on `iCloud.com`. You can't create a new group on any iOS device.

To add a new group on your Mac, open the **Contacts** app and go to **File | New Group**. You can also create a Smart Group; a group of contacts matching the conditions you decide, by navigating to **File | New Smart Group**.

Contacts on iCloud.com

Just like Mail, you can also access your iCloud Contacts directly from iCloud.com. Enter your iCloud account credentials, which are your Apple ID and password, to log in. Then, choose Contact and you will see a similar interface like that on iOS, as shown in the following screenshot:

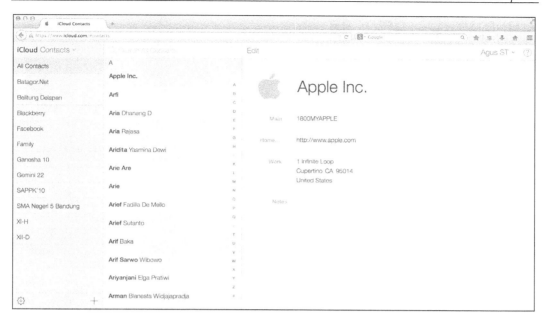

Calendar

iCloud also provides **Calendar** to let you add, edit, and manage events on your devices. Like **Contacts**, iCloud will automatically synchronize all events to your Mac, Windows PC, and iOS devices. That means you will get the same events and calendars available to all devices that have been linked with your iCloud account.

Make sure you've set the **Calendar** toggle to the ON position on iCloud preference panes in your Mac, or iCloud settings on your iOS devices to get the iCloud sync works.

Setting up calendars

In this section, you will learn how to add a new calendar or a new event on a Mac computer and iOS devices. Essentially, the steps you will follow on Mac are similar to that on iOS. So, you won't find any difficulties when you switch from Mac to iOS, or the reverse.

On your iOS devices

To view all iCloud calendars and events on your iOS device, open the **Calendar** app. To create a new calendar, go to **Calendars | Edit | Add calendar**. Then, you give a calendar name and change its label color.

To create a new event, click on the **+** button and a new screen opens up. Fill in all the information you have for your event. Click on the **Done** button when you've finished adding it to the **Calendar** and sync it to iCloud.

On your Mac

To view all of the iCloud calendars and events on your Mac, open the **Calendars** app (previously named iCal), as shown in the following screenshot. You can view the calendar in four different views: **Day, Week, Month**, and **Year**. Each view has a different interface depending on how you prefer to look at your agenda or events: by day, by week, by month, or by year:

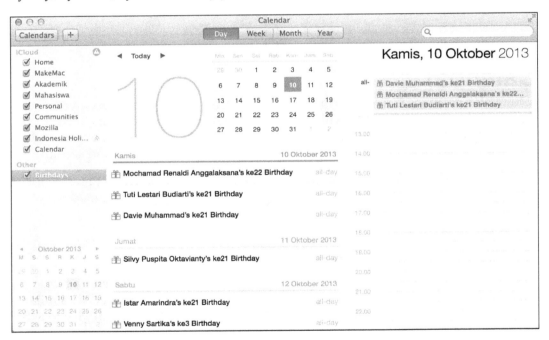

To create a new calendar, go to **File | New Calendar | iCloud** on the menu bar. A new calendar named **Untitled** will show up on the sidebar. You can rename it or change its label color by right-clicking on it and choosing **Get Info**. You can also add a description for the calendar.

To create a new event, click on the **+** button on the top-left corner and write a name for the event in a sentence, for example, Watching movie at 9 p.m. on Cinema Park. The **Calendar** app will automatically arrange a new event and its details based on your sentence. Don't forget to assign it to one of the iCloud calendars to sync it automatically to all devices.

Sharing your calendar with the public

It's super easy to share your calendar with your friends. They can subscribe it but they can't change any events because iCloud sets it as read-only version. To make a calendar public on your Mac, hover over the **Calendar** app and click on the **Share** button on the right. Check the **Public Calendar** checkbox to make it public.

You can also do it on your iOS device. Just click on the **i** icon beside the calendar name and set the **Public Calendar** toggle to the green position. Then, you can share the URL with your friends and let them subscribe to your calendar.

Calendar on iCloud.com

Just like **Mail** and **Contacts**, you also can access your **iCloud Calendar** directly from iCloud.com. Enter your iCloud account credentials, that is, your Apple ID and password to log in. Then, choose **Calendar** and you will see a similar interface like the **Calendar** app in iOS, as shown in the following screenshot:

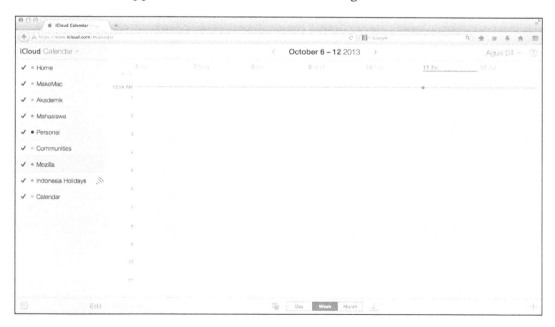

Summary

You've just learned how to configure the main services from iCloud that can help you gain some productivity on multiple devices. They are Mail, Contacts, and Calendar. These services can be accessed from the Mac computer, iOS devices, or even from any web browser via `iCloud.com`. iCloud helps you to sync all of content to all your configured devices. To learn how to configure these services on a Windows PC, refer to *Chapter 10, Using iCloud with Windows*.

In the next chapter, you'll be shown how to use iMessage, Notes, and Reminders.

4

Collaborate with iMessage, Notes, and Reminders

Apart from the three main features — Mail, Contacts, and Calendar — both OS X and iOS provide users with other services. In this chapter, we are going to explain more about iMessage, Notes, and Reminders. These services are also available on all of your devices associated with your Apple ID account. Except for iMessage, you can use them all with your Mac, iOS devices, and PC.

iMessage

Since the 2000s, most people have been able to communicate with their family or friends not only by voice calling, but also by sending them a **Short Message Service** (**SMS**) message, commonly known as a text message. SMS has become the cheaper alternative to voice calls for staying in touch.

In 2011, Apple introduced a service called iMessage that allows you to send messages over the Internet using Apple's private protocol. So, you can send messages between iOS devices and Macs using your current data plan or Wi-Fi anywhere in the world as long as you are connected to the Internet.

Sometimes people compare iMessage with **Blackberry Messenger** (**BBM**), but these apps actually have different approaches. iMessage treats all messages and forms of conversation like SMS, while BBM uses an ordinary instant messaging scheme — like that of Yahoo! Messenger — with a profile picture and status.

Setting up iMessage on your iOS device

Before using iMessage on iOS device, you need to activate it. iOS will automatically send a message via SMS to activate iMessage. iMessage is super easy to activate but may sometimes take time to be ready to use.

Activating iMessage

To start using iMessage on your iOS device, you need to set the **iMessage** toggle to the ON position first, under **Settings | Messages**, as shown in the following screenshot. Make sure that you have also logged into your iCloud account by navigating to **Settings | iCloud**:

Now, you can use the iMessage service to send messages for free over a data network. If you're using an iPhone or iPad with Wi-Fi + Cellular, make sure that your iPhone comes with a data plan, otherwise, you must be connected to a Wi-Fi network around you.

iMessage or SMS?

iMessage is integrated with the Messages app, and iOS will combine both SMS messages and iMessages with the same contacts. It's a good approach because you can track your conversation without installing or opening separate apps.

If your recipient has a phone number associated with an iMessage-enabled iOS device, you can send him or her an iMessage. For iPhone users, if your recipient is not an iOS device user and he or she hasn't enabled iMessage yet, the Messages app will automatically send it as an SMS message. In fact, messages that cannot be sent over iMessage for any reason — due to no network connection, for example — will be sent as text messages. A message sent over iMessage will be shown as a blue bubble, while a green bubble indicates that it's been sent as an SMS message.

More iMessage settings in iOS

There are several settings on how you can use and handle iMessage on your iOS devices. You can see them all by navigating to **Settings | Messages,** as shown in the following screenshot. We will now cover each of them to make sure you know how to use them:

- **Send Read Receipts**: Set the toggle to the ON position if you want allow others to be notified when you have read their messages. On their screen, the message will be marked **Read** and the time when you read it will also be displayed.

- **Send as SMS**: Set the toggle to the ON position to let iPhone send messages as SMS messages when iMessage is temporarily unavailable.

- **Send & Receive**: You can add and pick the e-mail addresses you want to link with your iOS devices to send and receive iMessage with.

Alerts and notifications for iMessage on iOS

Since iMessage is managed by the Messages app, all notifications—both for SMS messages and iMessage—use the same alert configuration. You can see it by navigating to **Settings | Notifications | Messages**. You can change how alerts are displayed and which tones are played as alerts for incoming text messages and iMessages.

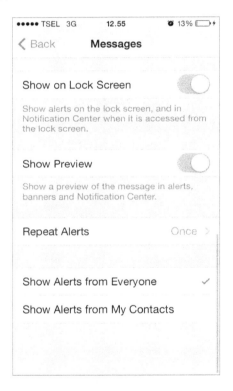

There's also an alert configuration specifically for iMessage: **Show iMessage Alerts From**. Just like its name suggests, this option lets you to decide whether you want to be notified about iMessages from just your saved contacts or from everyone, including people you don't know. It really helps you to filter iMessage based on saved contacts.

Setting up Messages on your Mac

As with iOS, iMessage is integrated to the Messages app in Mac, which was previously known as iChat. The Messages app is only available in OS X Mountain Lion (10.8.x).

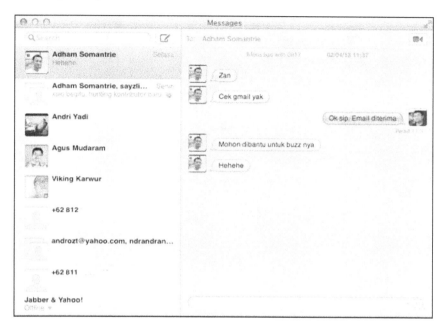

To start using iMessage on your Mac computer, you need to associate your Mac with an Apple ID. The simplest way to do this is by configuring your iCloud account to the iCloud preference pane. Then, OS X uses the iCloud e-mail address as the default account for iMessage. With the Messages app, all iMessages you've already sent and received are automatically synced and appear on the screen. Unfortunately, SMS messages won't be synced and will not appear here.

More iMessage settings for Mac

There are several settings for using and handling iMessage on your iOS devices. To check the Messages app preferences—including iMessage—on your Mac, you can go to **Messages** | **Preferences** | **Accounts**.

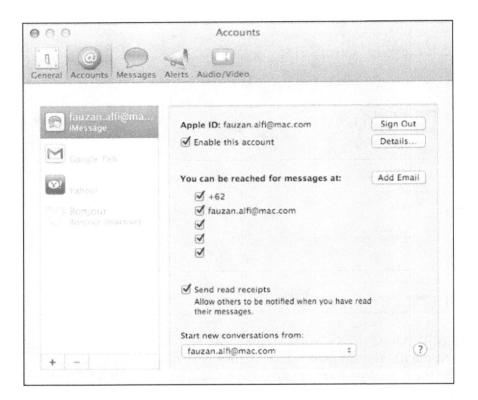

As shown in the preceding screenshot, you can configure your iMessage account. You can find most of the same options here as in iOS. Here, you can enable or disable your account for iMessage. You can also configure e-mail addresses that you want to use on sending and/or receiving incoming iMessages.

Beside iMessages, you can add new accounts for instant messaging, such as a Yahoo! Account for Yahoo! Messenger and a Google account for Google Talk. If you're familiar with iChat in older versions of OS X, you will know how to use it well.

Alerts and notifications for iMessage on Mac

You can also configure how Messages notifies you of new messages. Just go to **System Preferences | Notification**, choose **Messages**, and then choose an alert style, such as **Banners** or **Alerts**. You can also decide how many recent notifications you want to keep in the Notification Center, how many unread messages the badge app icon shows and the sound to play when your Mac receives notifications:

Since all messages are sent to all devices associated with an account, you will get a series of tones and notification beeps on your Mac and on your iOS devices simultaneously. I recommend that you to choose to receive all notifications for any new iMessages either on your Mac or on your iOS device.

Sending iMessages

Using iMessage, you are able to send text, but also pictures, location pins, and contact cards to any recipients—whether they are iMessage users or not. If sending for your iMessage fails for some reason, iMessage will fall back to SMS messages or MMS.

Sending texts

Sending text messages using iMessage is similar to sending SMS messages, which we are quite familiar with.

First, check the chatbox. If what's written is **iMessage** and the color of the **Send** button is blue, you can type and send your message as an iMessage.

Sending pictures

To send a picture as an iMessage in iOS, click on the camera button on the left-hand side of the chatbox. Then, choose whether you want to take a picture with the camera or pick a picture from the photo library. Pick the picture you want to send. You can add some text within the chatbox and tap the **Send** button, as shown in the following screenshot:

To send a picture as an iMessage in Mac, just drag and drop any pictures to the chatbox. Then, click on the **Send** button.

Sending a location pin

You can also send a location pin or location information to your friends over iMessage. It's useful when you want to inform your friend of a location for dinner, or arrange a meeting by just sending the location pin. Then with Maps, he or she can find your location, as shown in the following screenshot:

To send a location pin as an iMessage in iOS, you need to open the **Maps** app first. Tap the location on the map that you want to share. Click on the blue arrow, tap the **Share Location** button, and choose **Message**. You can add some text within the chatbox and then tap the **Send** button.

Sending contacts

To send a contact card as an iMessage in iOS, you need to open the **Contacts** app first Tap the contact you want to share. Tap the **Share Contact** button and choose **Message**. You can add some text within the chatbox then, tap the **Send** button.

To send a contact card as an iMessage in OS X, you need to open the **Contacts** app first, as shown in the preceding screenshot. Choose a contact you want to share, and then click on the **Share** button on the bottom left-hand corner of the right-hand pane. Choose **Message Card** and a compose window will show up within the app. You can add recipients and some text within the chatbox and then tap the **Send** button.

Notes

Notes is the simplest app on Apple devices to keep all of your important notes, simple task lists, or even recipes, and all notes are synchronized to the iCloud server. So, all your notes are available to see on all of your devices authenticated with the same iCloud account.

Notes on your iOS device

Since the introduction of iPhone and iOS, Notes has been the default app for note taking. To create a note, you can open the Notes app and press the **+** button in the top right-hand corner of the screen. If your iOS device has Siri on it, you can create a note just by dictating. By default, all your Notes are saved to iCloud.

Sharing a note on iOS

You also can share your notes just by tapping the share icon at the bottom of the screen (next to the trash button). You can share it by e-mail, iMessage, or directly print it to any AirPrint-enabled printing machine.

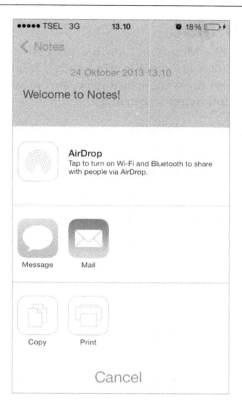

Configuring Notes on iOS

You can change your default account to save and synchronize your notes by navigating to **Settings | Notes,** as shown in the following screenshot. By default, it is **iCloud**:

Notes on your Mac

Since Apple introduced OS X Mountain Lion, a similar Notes app has been available as a built-in app and the notes are synchronized with iCloud. To create a new note, just open the **Notes** app and press the **+** button on the bottom left-hand corner of the window as shown in the following screenshot:

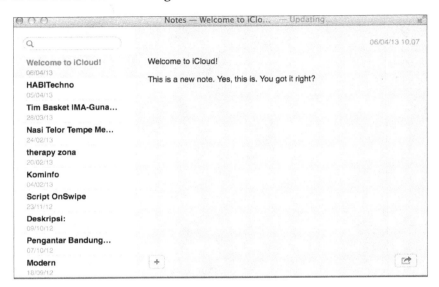

Since Notes supports rich text editing, you can add pictures to your notes. Simply drag-and-drop any picture to a note; it'll appear in your Note and will be synchronized with all of your Apple devices. By default, all of your notes are saved to iCloud.

Sharing a note on Mac

You also can share your notes just by clicking on the share icon at the bottom of the screen (next to the trash button). You can share it by e-mail and iMessage. To print it, you need to go to **File | Print**.

Configuring Notes on Mac

Just like in iOS, you're also able to change the font of Notes by navigating to **Format | Fonts | Default Fonts**, where you can choose one of three available fonts: **Noteworthy**, **Helvetica**, and **Market Felt**. You can also use any fonts available on your Mac. To configure your default account for Notes, you can go to **Notes | Accounts**, and you will be redirected to the **Mail, Contacts & Calendar** preference pane under **System Preferences**.

Notes on iCloud.com

Notes is also parts of the iCloud web application. If you don't have your devices with you, you can access all of your synchronized notes from the Web:

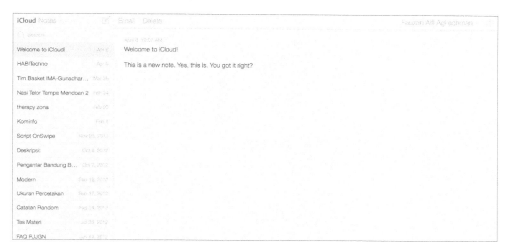

For Notes, there are no big differences between native apps on OS X or iOS and web apps on `iCloud.com`. You can create a new note, share it by e-mail, or delete a note directly from the Notes web app.

To trash it or not; that's the question

If you want to delete a note in Notes, make sure that you really want to delete it forever. Why? Because once it's deleted, Notes automatically synchronizes with the iCloud server and deletes the note permanently.

Reminders

With Reminders, you can create and group to-do lists from your Apple devices. Just like others, all to-do lists created with Reminders are automatically synchronized to all of your devices authenticated with the same iCloud account.

Reminders on iOS devices

To create a new reminder list, tap the "three lines" button in the top left-hand corner of the screen, tap **Edit**, and then tap **Create New List...**. Type the name for a new reminder list, and if finished, tap **Done**. Then, you can create a new reminder inside the list by clicking on the **+** button in the top right-hand corner of the screen.

In iOS, tap any reminder and a detail screen is displayed. You can modify any parameters for your reminder here.

There are some parameters you can change, which are explained as follows:

- **Remind Me On a Day**: You can set the reminder to alert you on any date you want or after a specific period of time.

- **Remind Me At a Location**: Reminders helps you to set up alerts based on your location. You can pick whether you want your alerts to pop up when leaving or arriving at a specific location.

- **Priority**: You can set a reminder to high (!!!), medium (!!), or low (!) priority.

- **List**: You can move the reminder from one list to another.

- **Notes**: Add some notes related to reminders if needed.

Reminders on Mac

Before iCloud was officially launched, Reminders was integrated with iCal—a default calendar and to-do list management app for OS X. When OS X Mountain Lion was released, Apple created a separate app for to-do list management called Reminders.

To create a new reminder list, press the **+** button in the bottom left-hand corner of the window. Then, you can create a new reminder inside the list by clicking on the **+** button in the top right-hand corner of the window. To modify a reminder on Mac, hover over any reminder / to-do item and click on the **i** button (information button).

Reminders on iCloud.com

Reminders is also part of iCloud web applications. If you don't have your devices with you, you can access all of your synchronized to-do lists and reminders that you've created from the Web.

For Reminders, there are no big differences between native apps on iOS and web apps on iCloud.com, while you get a different interface on OS X. You can create a new reminder or reminder list, modify it, add an alert, or add a priority level on a reminder directly from the Reminders web app.

Summary

You've learned about iMessage, Notes, and Reminders and how to use them properly on your devices. iMessage helps you to send messages or other files using your data plan or via a wireless network. Basically, it lets you send files for free. Notes lets you write any important notes, and you can add pictures into the notes. Reminders helps you to remember any event or to-do lists you must complete in a period of time or at a location. So far, those three services help you to collaborate with your friends, colleagues, or even your family.

In the next chapter, we will learn how iCloud is integrated with iPhoto and iTunes services.

5
Using iPhoto and iTunes with iCloud

When you have more than one iOS device and love capturing moments with your devices, the **Photo Stream** app might be the most useful feature for you on iCloud. Photo Stream stores all of the pictures that you captured with your devices. It includes all of the pictures you've taken using the Camera app and also the screenshots from your iOS devices. So, you don't need to resynchronize or resend pictures from one device to another. They're automatically there for you.

Photo Stream

The way that Photo Stream works is really simple. First, you take some pictures using your iOS device. Then, these pictures are automatically uploaded to the iCloud server. Other devices that have Photo Stream enabled receive these pictures immediately. Photo Stream only stores pictures that are taken using the Camera app on iOS devices.

Of course, your devices need to be connected to the Internet via cellular data or Wi-Fi. For those who use Wi-Fi-only iOS devices, such as iPod touch and iPad with Wi-Fi, pictures are uploaded later when it's connected to Internet.

Photo Stream lets you upload unlimited pictures and it won't count on iCloud storage, but these are stored in Photo Stream for 30 days. After that, your pictures are automatically deleted. Make sure that you have stored all pictures on your Mac or PC so that you don't lose any. All pictures are uploaded in full resolution, but when they are downloaded to iOS devices, the resolution is reduced and optimized for the devices.

Setting up Photo Stream

All Mac computers with OS X Lion or higher, PCs with an iCloud Control Panel, and iOS devices with iOS 5 or higher are able to store and receive pictures from Photo Stream. To use Photo Stream on your device, you need to activate it on each device. So, you can also decide on which devices you want to store and receive pictures using Photo Stream.

Photo Stream on iOS

It's hard for me (and maybe for you too), if I don't enable Photo Stream on my iPhone because Photo Stream is the easiest way to share pictures and screenshots across iOS devices. You don't need to share them by e-mail or using other apps. Just let iCloud stream them to all devices.

To enable Photo Stream on iOS, navigate to **Settings** | **Photos & Camera**. Set the **My Photo Stream** toggle to the ON position, as shown in the preceding screenshot, and that's all! Photo Stream is now ready to serve you. You can also enable Photo Stream by navigating to **Settings** | **iCloud** | **Photo Stream** and setting the **My Photo Stream** toggle to the ON position. To view all pictures stored on Photo Stream, you need to open the Photos app, tap on the **Albums** tab, and then tap on the **My Photo Stream** tab at the bottom of the screen. You can browse and view the pictures just like browsing pictures on Albums or Events, as shown in the following screenshot:

You can share pictures from Photo Stream to Mail, Message, Twitter, or Facebook; many other actions are available as well. You can also delete pictures individually from Photo Stream. Tap on **Select** and tap on the pictures that you want to delete. Then, tap on the **Delete** icon to execute the process.

Saving pictures from Photo Stream to Camera Roll is really easy. Just tap on **Select** and choose the pictures that you want to save. If you're finished, tap on the **Share** icon and choose the **Save to Camera Roll** icon at the bottom of the screen to store all chosen pictures to Camera Roll. You must choose whether to keep the pictures in an existing album or in a new album.

Photo Stream on Mac

Photo Stream on Mac is really great. It's integrated with iPhoto; one of the applications in iLife suite for managing photos and videos. You will have it installed by default when you purchase a new Mac, or you can purchase it by yourself via the Mac App Store. With iPhoto, you can add and delete pictures in Photo Stream. One big advantage of having Photo Stream enabled on your Mac is that you don't need to plug in your iOS device to your Mac just for copying pictures taken with it.

To enable Photo Stream on Mac, navigate to **System Preferences | iCloud** and check the **Photos** checkbox to enable it. You can manage and view your Photo Stream on iPhoto or Aperture. You can also use pictures from Photo Stream on iMovie as part of Media Browser.

Viewing Photo Stream on iPhoto

After you've enabled Photo Stream from the iCloud preference pane, launch iPhoto on your Mac. You'll see the **iCloud** icon on the left sidebar. Click on it and iPhoto shows a welcome screen, as shown in the following screenshot. Click on **Turn On iCloud** to enable Photo Stream, and iPhoto will download all pictures stored on Photo Stream automatically. It usually takes longer to download Photo Stream pictures for the first time:

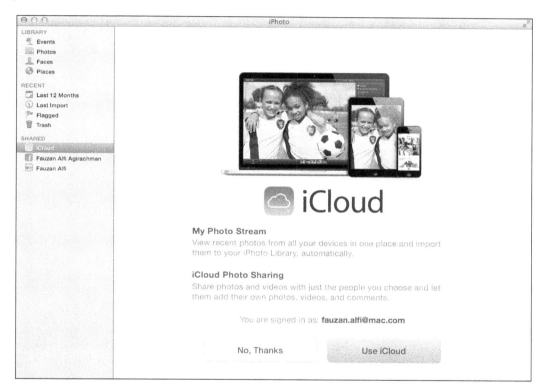

Photo Stream on iPhoto has different behaviors compared to Photo Stream on iOS. All Photo Stream pictures, which have been downloaded to iPhoto, are automatically stored in your iPhoto Library. It's not only stored but also organized with iPhoto as Event. So, you'll see something like "Jan 2013 Photo Stream", which contains Photo Stream pictures from January 2013.

Pictures from Photo Stream behave like other pictures on iPhoto. These are available on Media Browser, which is connected with other apps on your Mac. Everything is organized so there is no more dragging and dropping from your mobile device to your Mac.

By default, every new picture added to your iPhoto Library is uploaded to Photo Stream. You can disable it by navigating to **iPhoto | Preferences | iCloud** and unchecking **Automatic Upload**, as shown in the following screenshot:

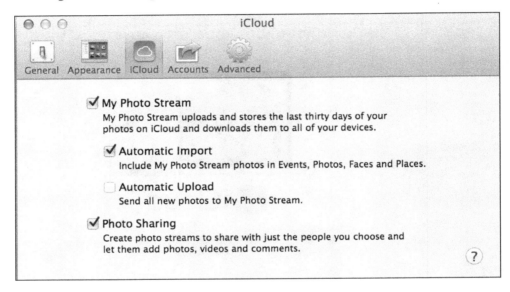

Photo Sharing

If you're familiar with **MobileMe Gallery**, you're going to see similarities with this feature. **Photo Sharing** is the best way to share your pictures with your friends, family, or even everybody on the Internet.

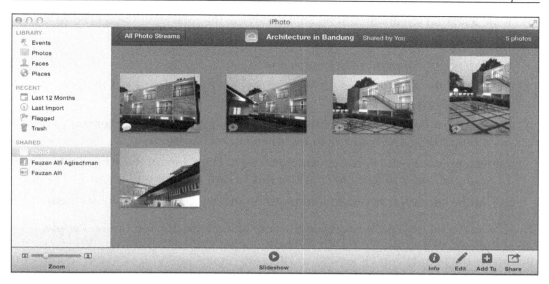

You can create a new shared stream on iPhoto from your Mac or on the Photos app from your iOS device. You can decide who is able to see your shared pictures or even share a public link, and anyone with an Apple device can see your pictures.

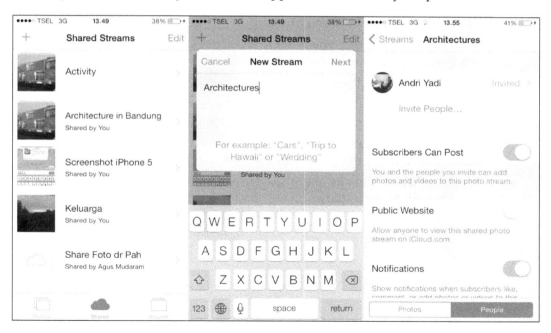

To create a shared stream album on an iOS device, the following steps need to be performed:

1. Tap on the **Shared** tab in Photos app.

2. Tap on the **+** button and name your new shared stream. After that, tap on **Next**.

3. In the **To** field, add your friends' iCloud e-mail addresses. Enter the album title in the **Name** field and then tap on **Create**.

4. Tap on your newly created shared stream. Then, tap on the **+** button to add pictures you want to share on this stream and tap on **Done**.

5. Add a caption for your shared pictures and tap on **Post** to publish them.

If you want to set up a public website for your shared stream, tap on the **People** tab at the bottom and set the **Public Website** toggle to the ON position. You can also allow the people you've invited to add new photos and videos to the stream by setting the **Subscribers Can Post** toggle to the ON position.

To create a shared stream album on your Mac, the following steps need to be performed:

1. Choose the pictures you want to share from iPhoto Library. Then, click on **Share** and choose **New Photo Stream**.

2. iPhoto asks you whether you want to share the same pictures that are already stored on your Library. Click on **Show in Library**.

3. Click on **New Photo Stream**.

4. In the **To** textbox, add your friends' iCloud e-mail addresses. Enter the album title in the **Name** field.

5. Check the **Subscribers Can Post** checkbox if you want to allow the subscribers to add more photos and videos to your shared stream.

6. Check the **Public Website** checkbox if you want to share it publicly. Then, click on **Next** to share.

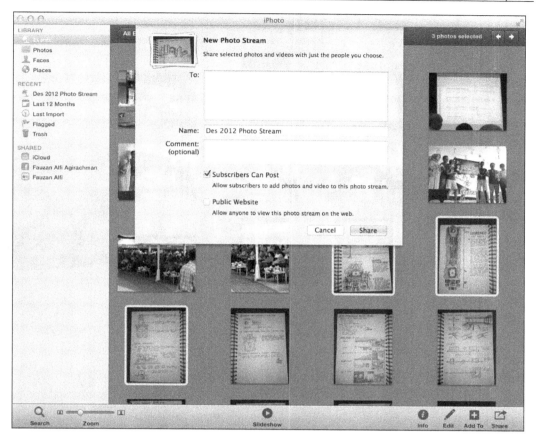

On the shared stream, both you and your invited friends will be able to add comments or like the shared pictures. It has an interface similar to that of the photo album on Facebook. Now with iOS 7 and the latest version of iPhoto, your friends can post new photos and videos to the stream.

iTunes in the Cloud

One of the reasons for having Apple devices is the iTunes Store. This store offers you lots of music, movies, apps, podcasts, and books that can be purchased or downloaded directly from your Apple devices. Since iCloud came out, Apple integrated iTunes Store content as part of the iCloud service. It's called **iTunes in the Cloud**.

Earlier, when you needed to synchronize your devices to get the same content that you've bought from the iTunes Store—whether it was music, movies, or even apps—and also when you tried to download content that you had already purchased on your iOS device, you would be charged again with the same price.

Now, iTunes in the Cloud keeps your purchased list and lets you download them all over again directly from your devices. You can also configure to automatically download content you've purchased to all of your devices.

iTunes in the Cloud supports music, movies, TV shows, podcasts, books, and apps. I recommend that you should use the latest version of iOS, OS X, and the iTunes app to get the best experience.

Purchased music

The iTunes Store has lots of music ready to be purchased and downloaded. It's now DRM-free and available in **iTunes Plus** with bit rate quality of 128 Kbps. With iCloud, iTunes Store lets you download purchased music directly to your device.

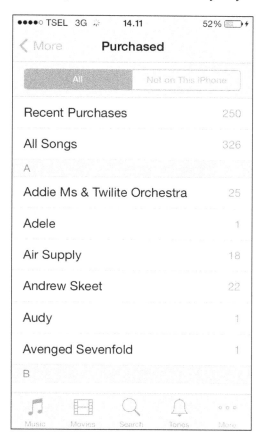

To see your purchased music list on an iOS device, navigate to **iTunes | More | Purchased | Music**. You can see the recent music you've purchased and all purchased music with the artist list. iTunes Store also lets you to see purchased music that's not in your iOS device yet. Tap on **Not on this iPhone** (depending on your iOS device) to see them. To download a purchased song, tap on the cloud icon beside the song title.

To see your purchased music list on Mac, navigate to **iTunes | Music**. You can see the purchased music that's not on your Mac yet. To download it, click on the cloud button beside the song title.

Purchased music on Apple TV

On Apple TV with Software Update 6 or higher, you can purchase music from your Apple TV and listen to it directly by streaming on your TV. You need to log in to your iTunes Store account on your Apple TV. Then, go back to the home screen and launch Music. Since it's streaming music, you need a stable Internet connection for your Apple TV.

Purchased movies

The iTunes Store lets you purchase or rent lots of movies. Most movies are available both on SD and HD quality. With iCloud, iTunes Store lets you download purchased movies directly to your device.

To see your purchased movies list on an iOS device, navigate to **iTunes | More | Purchased | Movie**. You can see a list of purchased movies here. The iTunes Store also lets you see the purchased movies that are not on your iOS device yet. Tap on **Not on this iPhone** (depending on your iOS device) to see them. To download a purchased movie, tap on the movie you want to download and tap on the cloud icon near the movie title.

To see the purchased movies on Mac, navigate to **iTunes | Movie**. You can see your purchased movies that are not on your Mac yet with iCloud icon on its cover. To download them, click on the cloud icon beside the song title.

Purchased movies on Apple TV

Similar to purchased music, you can enjoy purchasing movies and watching them directly by streaming to your TV. You need to log in to your iTunes Store account on your Apple TV. Then, go back to the home screen and launch Movie. To get the best experience, you need a stable broadband Internet connection when streaming the movie on your Apple TV.

Purchased apps

With the App Store, iTunes offers you lots of great apps and has the largest mobile apps library so far. The iPhone app, iPad app, and also the universal app are all available for purchase and download here. With iCloud, the iTunes Store lets you download purchased apps directly to your device.

To see your purchased app list on an iOS device, navigate to **App Store | Updates | Purchased**. The iTunes Store also lets you see purchased apps that are not on your iOS device yet. Tap on **Not on this iPhone** (depending on your iOS device) to see them. To download a purchased app, tap on the cloud icon beside the app title, as shown in the following screenshot:

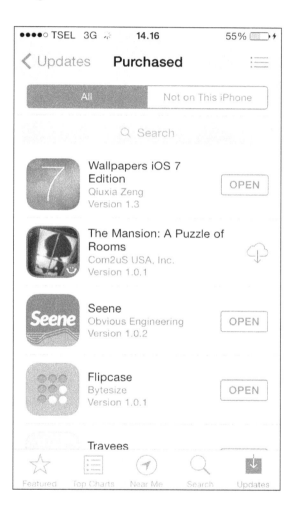

To see your purchased app list on Mac, navigate to **iTunes | iTunes Store | App Store**. Click on **Purchased** on the left sidebar of the App Store. To download a purchased app, click on the cloud icon beside the app title.

iTunes Match

What is **iTunes Match**? It's a subscription service from Apple and it stores your entire iTunes music library on iCloud. So, you can access and listen to your entire music library wherever you are. iTunes Match works not only for the music you've purchased from the iTunes Store, but also for the music that you've purchased from other sources, including music imported from a CD. iTunes Match also lets you download higher a quality of your current songs for free.

iTunes Match makes it easier for you to listen to any music on your library, without syncing it first to your Mac or PC. Since it's streaming music from the Internet, make sure you have a stable Internet connection, or that you've subscribed to a cellular data plan for your iPhone.

To use this service, you will have to pay USD 24.99 per year in the United States, at the time of writing this book. Prices may vary in other countries and can be changed from time to time. Just like in my country, Indonesia, iTunes Match costs about IDR 199,000 per year. To check whether iTunes Match is available for your country and how much it costs, just open iTunes, then click on **Music** in the left menu, and click on the **Match** tab. A complete list of iTunes Match availability can be found at http://support. apple.com/kb/ht5085.

You can set up iTunes Match in up to five devices with the same account.

Setting up iTunes Match

You can set up and subscribe to iTunes Match on your Mac or PC. Navigate to **iTunes | Music | Match,** and the iTunes Match page will be opened. Click on the **Subscribe for [COST] per year** button (where [COST] is the most recent iTunes Match price for your country) to subscribe and then you'll be prompted to enter your Apple ID and password. Then, click on **Subscribe**.

After that, iTunes Match starts the matching process in three steps: gathering information about your iTunes Library, matching them with songs in the iTunes Store, and uploading artwork and the remaining songs. In step 3, iTunes uploads all of the music from your Library that still doesn't exist in the iTunes Store and you can still listen to the entire Library anywhere.

If you add new songs from sources other than the iTunes Store, you can refresh iTunes Match by navigating to **Store | Update iTunes Match**.

Using iTunes Match on iOS

To enable iTunes Match on an iOS device, navigate to **Settings | iTunes & App Stores** and set the **iTunes Match** toggle to the ON position. Then, enter your Apple ID and password and tap on **Enable** to replace your current Music Library on the iOS device with iTunes Match library.

To use iTunes Match on iOS, your device must be connected to the Internet because it streams your library directly from cloud. You can also download any music and store it permanently just by tapping on the cloud icon.

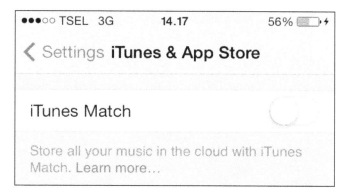

Using iTunes Match on Mac

To enable iTunes Match on Mac, navigate to **Store | Turn On iTunes Match** and iTunes connects to the server to check whether an empty slot for your Mac is available. Make sure that you've logged in with your iTunes Store account with the iTunes Match subscription. Then, the iTunes Match screen is shown (like the one shown in the following screenshot). Click on **Add This Computer** button. iTunes will ask you to input your Apple ID and password. After that, iTunes Match is ready to serve.

Using iTunes Match on Apple TV

To enable iTunes Match on Apple TV, navigate to **Settings | iTunes Store | iTunes Match**. Click it once with your Apple Remote to turn it ON. Now you can listen and stream your entire music library by opening the Music app on Apple TV.

Summary

With Photo Stream, every single picture saved in Camera Roll is uploaded to the iCloud server and made available to all of your devices. Then, you can share these pictures with your friends and loved ones by creating a Shared Photo Stream and let them comment or like the pictures. You will have no more hassle sending images via e-mail or sharing using USB just for showing the pictures to the people you want.

On the other hand, iTunes in the Cloud helps you to access and redownload all your purchased content without extra charge. Once you have bought a movie on your iPhone, you can enjoy it later on your Mac at home. Thanks to the Automatic Downloads feature on iTunes which is a part of iTunes in the Cloud. Same thing happens to your other purchased contents. Even with iTunes Match, you can have your iTunes Library with you everywhere, since it's already available on the iCloud server.

6
Syncing Your Contents with iCloud

Besides purchased content, e-mails, contacts, and calendars, iCloud also stores your other documents such as text documents, spreadsheets, and presentations. Unlike other services, iCloud also syncs your documents. It's really useful if you work on multiple devices. You don't need to transfer the files from one device to another. Just let iCloud do the synchronization bit, and you get the most recent files on any device. This feature is known as **Documents in the Cloud**.

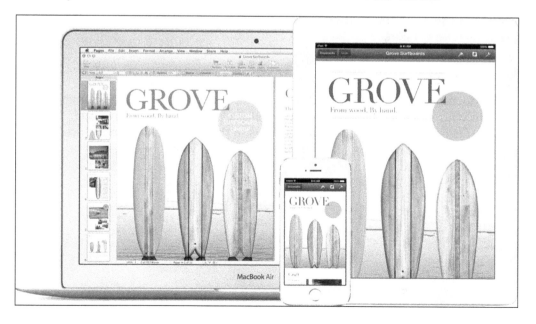

Documents in the Cloud

Documents in the Cloud works with Mac or iOS apps that are compatible with the service. It automatically syncs your documents and data to the cloud and shares them with all of your devices. Everything happens almost instantaneously except in Windows PCs, where you need to manually sync it. Apple only supports document synchronization on Mac computers that are iCloud-enabled and on iOS devices.

Syncing iWork Documents with iCloud

By default, iCloud natively syncs documents created by iWork—Apple's own productivity software suite. iWork includes Pages for word processing, Numbers for spreadsheets, and Keynote for presentations. iCloud syncs between iWork apps for Mac and iOS. All the synced documents are available on each device based on the document type.

All documents synced by iWork are also available on the `icloud.com` website. You can view them by opening the related iWork web apps, Pages, Numbers, and Keynotes. Now, you can even edit your documents directly on the Web without having to possess or use native iWork apps on your computer. Even though these web apps are still in beta, they are quite stable and match the functionality of their native iOS app counterpart. At the time of writing this book, it's still unknown when Apple plans to remove the beta label and release the final version.

Syncing documents on iOS devices

To sync documents from the iCloud server to iOS devices, you need to enable iCloud in your device as explained in *Chapter 2*, *Getting Started with iCloud*. Then, you need to make sure that Documents in the Cloud is enabled. Once you enable it, any supporting app, including iWork for iOS, will be able to sync documents to iCloud.

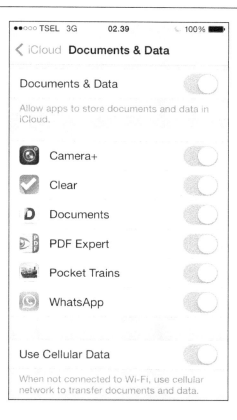

To enable the Documents in the Cloud feature on an iOS device, perform the following steps:

1. Open **Settings** from the home screen.

2. Tap on **iCloud**.

3. Then tap on **Documents & Data**.

4. Then, set the **Documents & Data** toggle to the ON position. Once you have set it, supporting apps start to store documents to the iCloud server.

5. If you have a device with its cellular data network enabled, you can set the **Use Cellular Data** toggle to the ON position in order to sync documents on the go over the cellular data network. It's better to set it to OFF if your cellular data plan is limited to avoid downloading data over quota.

Syncing documents on Mac

To sync documents from the iCloud server to your Mac computer, you need to associate your device with an iCloud account as explained in *Chapter 2, Getting Started With iCloud*. Then you need to make sure **Documents & Data** is enabled. Once you enable it, any supporting app, including iWork for Mac or TextEdit, will be able to sync their documents to the iCloud.

To enable the Documents in the Cloud feature on your Mac, perform the following steps:

1. Open **System Preferences**.
2. Click on the **iCloud** preference pane.
3. Click on **Documents & Data**.
4. Then check the **Documents & Data** checkbox. Once you've done this, supporting apps start to store documents to the iCloud server.

Syncing data from third-party apps

Apple allows third-party apps to use the Documents to the Cloud feature for saving documents, such as text documents for the note-taking app, or even for saving the sessions and achievements of games. All data and documents are uploaded to the cloud and downloaded back to other devices.

 If you're curious about what kind of data and documents are stored on your iCloud account, you can visit http://developer.icloud.com and click on **Documents** to find out more.

The Safari web browser

iCloud keeps your Safari bookmarks and Reading List up-to-date across all of your devices. There's also the iCloud tabs that show all of the web pages you have open on your iPad, iPhone, iPod touch, and Mac, so you can pick up browsing wherever you left it. Safari saves the whole content of the web pages—not just links—in your Reading List, so you can open the web page on any device, even when you're not connected to the Internet.

Enabling sync for Safari on iOS

To enable sync for Safari on an iOS device, perform the following steps:

1. Open the **Settings** app.
2. Tap on **iCloud**.

3. Set the **Safari** (or **Bookmarks** on an iOS 5 device) toggle to the ON position. This automatically syncs the bookmarks, Reading List, and tabs on Safari.

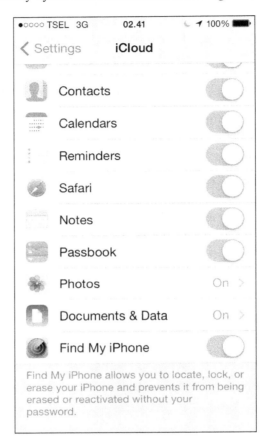

Enabling sync for Safari on Mac

To enable sync for Safari on a Mac, perform the following steps:

1. Open **System Preferences**.
2. Click on the **iCloud** preference pane.
3. Click on the **Safari** (or **Bookmarks** on OS X Lion) checkbox. It automatically syncs the bookmarks, Reading List, and tabs on Safari.

Syncing bookmarks

Once you've enabled sync for Safari, iCloud automatically syncs bookmarks on your Mac and iOS devices. You will get the same bookmarks on any device. Be careful—if you delete a bookmark from one device, it's also deleted on the other devices.

On Mac, iCloud syncs all of the bookmarks stored inside Safari for Mac. It includes bookmarks on the bookmarks bar and menu. On iOS, iCloud syncs all the bookmarks stored inside Safari for iOS.

To see all the synced bookmarks on Safari for Mac, go to **Bookmarks | Show All Bookmarks** or click on the book-like logo at the top left-hand side of Safari.

To see all the synced bookmarks on Safari for iOS, open **Safari** and tap on the bookmarks logo on the bottom bar.

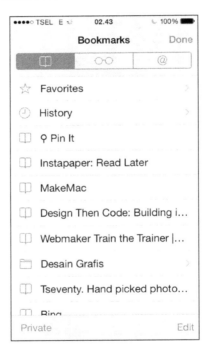

Syncing iCloud Tabs between devices

Since iOS 6 and Mountain Lion, Apple lets you sync a set of tabs you've opened on any of your devices. iCloud saves the latest set of tabs and syncs them to the other iCloud devices. It's called **iCloud Tabs**. It's very useful for those who are viewing some web pages on a Mac, for instance, and want to view the same pages again on an iOS device. iCloud also saves a different set of tabs from different devices. It shows your device's name as a label to recognize the devices that the set of tabs come from.

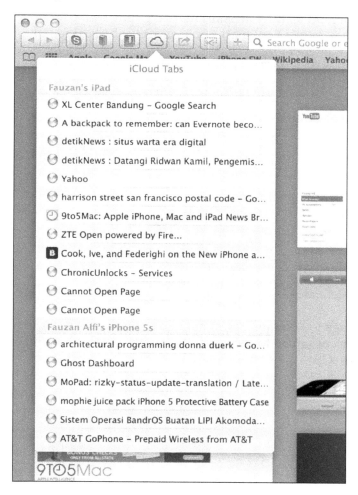

To see iCloud Tabs on Safari for Mac, just click on the iCloud icon on the toolbar and a pop-up window appears. Click on any web page title to open it as a new tab on Safari. To see iCloud Tabs on Safari for iOS, tap the Bookmarks icon on the bottom bar and then tap on **iCloud Tabs**. Tap any website title to open it as a new page on Safari.

Syncing Reading List

If you're familiar with Instapaper or the Pocket app, Reading List is not really different. It's a default feature on Safari that saves any web pages that you want to view again later. While Bookmarks only saves the web page links, Reading List saves the whole content of the web page, so you can view it later even when there is no Internet connection. Offline Reading List is available on iOS 6 or later.

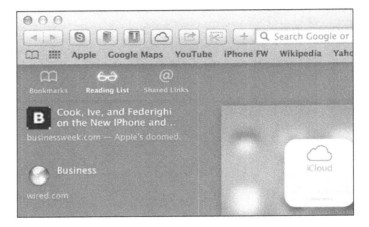

To add a web page to Reading List, simply go to **Bookmarks** | **Add to Reading List** on Safari for Mac, or tap on the **Share** button on the bottom bar and tap on **Add to Reading List** for iOS.

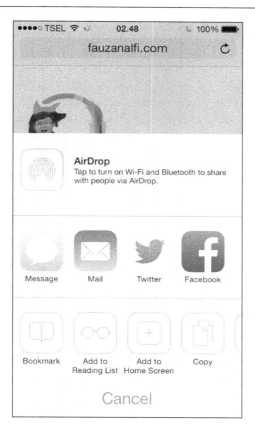

You can view all saved web pages on Reading List just by clicking on the glasses icon on Mac or go to **Bookmarks | Reading Lists** on iOS.

iBooks

iBooks is an app made by Apple that lets you read e-books on your iOS devices, and also on Mac with OS X Mavericks (v10.9). It supports e-books with the `.epub` extension and PDF documents. Inside the iBooks app for iOS, Apple offers fiction and non-fiction books on its own iBookstore. You can also purchase books from well-known publishers around the world. For some countries, you can download most of the free classic books.

Purchased iBooks

To see your purchased books list on an iOS device, open the **iBooks** app. It's not pre-installed, so you need to install it manually from the AppStore. Then, go to **Store | Purchased**. You can see all of your purchased books. The iBookstore also lets you see the purchased books that are not on your iOS device yet. Tap on **Not on this iPhone** (depends on your iOS device) to see them. To download a purchased book, tap on the Cloud button next to the app title, as shown in the following screenshot:

To see your purchased books list on Mac, go to **iTunes | iTunes Store | Books**. Click on the **Purchased** tab on the left sidebar of books. To download a purchased book, click on the Cloud icon next to the app title.

Syncing bookmarks on iBooks

Reading iBooks on an iPhone or iPad is fun and interactive. For people who have more than one iOS device, they sometimes start reading a book on one device and then continue on another device.

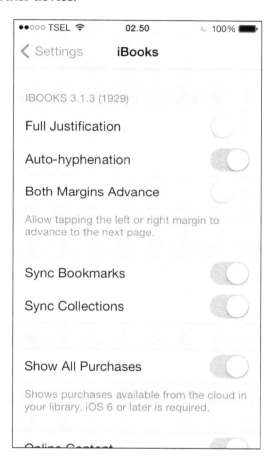

By syncing the bookmarks on iBooks, you can get the same bookmarks of the same book on all of the devices. So, you can continue reading your favorite book anywhere.

To enable the bookmarks sync on iBooks, perform the following steps:

1. Open the **Settings** app on your iOS device.

2. Tap on **iBooks**.

3. Set the **Sync Bookmarks** toggle to the ON position in order to sync all of the bookmarks on iBooks.

Summary

iCloud makes most of your documents, content, and data available on all your devices, even your bookmarks or the last state on a game. With Documents in the Cloud, all your documents are available to be accessed from all devices, including iWork documents on each iWork app. Documents on third-party apps are also synchronized to iCloud as long as they support the Documents in the Cloud service. Bookmarks, history, and Reading List on the Safari web browser are also synced through all devices.

7
Exploring iCloud Apps

In the previous chapter, we learned how to use the Documents in the Cloud feature within supported apps on Mac and iOS devices. In earlier chapters, we've seen some iCloud.com web apps such as Mail, Contacts, and Calendars. Now, we're going to see what more we can do in iCloud.com to support our productivity on multi-devices.

iCloud.com

The website iCloud.com is the place where you can see all of your data stored in iCloud. It also has seven web apps, which are Mail, Contacts, Calendars, Notes, Reminders, Find My iPhone, and iWork, that you can access from any modern desktop web browser. In order to properly access iCloud.com, Apple requires the following web browsers and minimum versions: Safari 5, Firefox 21, Google Chrome 27, or Internet Explorer 9. You also cannot access it from Safari on iOS devices.

In mobile Safari, instead of the iCloud login window, you will be redirected to the iCloud website for iOS that guides you on setting up iCloud on the device or installing the Find My iPhone or Find My Friends app.

To use web apps on iCloud.com, visit www.icloud.com using any supported web browser available on Mac or PC. Enter your iCloud credentials and then iCloud.com is ready to use.

Change iCloud.com settings

On iCloud.com, there are some settings that you can change to personalize your profile, such as your profile picture, language, and time zone. To change these, perform the following steps:

1. On the iCloud home screen, click on your name at the top-right corner of the web app.

2. To add or change your picture, click on the picture box, then click on **Choose Photo**. A file upload dialog will open. Select a picture that you want from your computer and then click on **Open**. You can drag the slider to adjust the zoom level of your picture. You can also drag it to crop it. If it's done, click on the **Done** button.

3. To change the language on the iCloud.com interface, click on **Language** and select any available language.

4. To change your time zone, click on **Time Zone**. Click on any time zone area on the map or click on the city name to choose from any of the cities in the pop-up menu, as shown in the following screenshot:

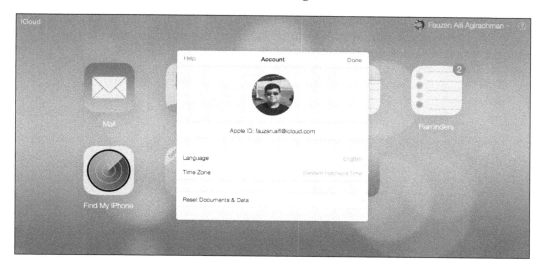

Notifications on iCloud.com

The website iCloud.com also shows any notifications at the top of the window. It supports notifications from Mail, Calendar, Reminders, and Find My iPhone. In the latest version of iCloud.com, you can't change any of the settings for notifications in the web app.

Find My iPhone

From all the services and features that are available on iCloud, this may be the coolest one ever. Find My iPhone is a service that helps you to find your iOS device and Mac computers wherever they are. On Mac, this feature is known as Find My Mac.

In most cases, the police and users find missing or stolen iOS devices using Find My iPhone. You can also track down the iOS device's movements when it's lost, or even send sound and message alerts to it.

To use Find My iPhone, you need to configure it on each iOS device and Mac computer. Then, you can track them down using the Find My iPhone app on iCloud.com or any iOS device.

Configure Find My iPhone on iOS devices

The Find My iPhone service uses location services that are supported on iOS 2 or later, but this service itself has been available since iOS 3.1.3 or later. It determines the location of your iOS devices based on the triangulation of cellular data location and Wi-Fi networks, if available. If your iOS devices are not connected to the Internet, you can't track your device.

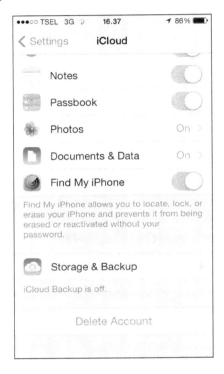

To use Find My iPhone, you need to perform the following steps:

1. Go to **Settings | iCloud**.
2. Scroll down the screen. Then set the **Find My iPhone** or **Find My iPod touch** or **Find My iPad** toggle to the ON position.

Configure Find My Mac on Mac

Just like Find My iPhone on iOS, the Find My Mac service uses Location Services that are supported on OS X 10.7 Lion or later. It determines the location of your Mac based on nearby Wi-Fi networks or cellular networks if you use any GSM mobile modems. If your Mac doesn't have Wi-Fi capabilities, you can't find your Mac using iCloud even if it's connected to the Internet via an Ethernet port.

To use Find My Mac, you need to perform the following instructions:

1. Open **System Preferences**, then click on the **iCloud** preference pane.
2. Click on the **Find My Mac** checkbox to activate this setting. Click on **Yes** if you are prompted.

Find your Apple devices

Once your devices are configured, iCloud determines the location of your devices using Location Services and displays this on the Find My iPhone app. You can track it using iCloud.com or the app itself. For this chapter, I'm going to use iCloud.com instead of the Find My iPhone app.

To find and track your device using iCloud.com, you need to perform the following instructions:

1. Browse to iCloud.com on the desktop web browser.

2. If iCloud doesn't show you all the available apps, and instead shows the web app that was last used, click on the cloud button on the top left-hand corner of the window to get back to the iCloud.com home screen.

3. Click on the Find My iPhone icon.

4. Enter your iCloud account password if prompted.

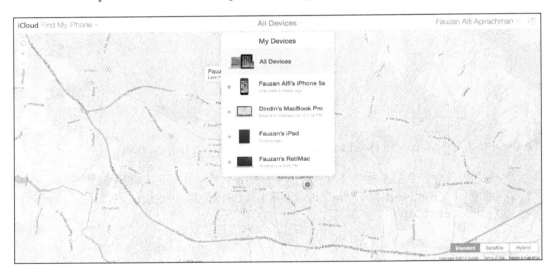

Find My iPhone shows you a map with dots that represent your devices. The green dots represent the currently connected/detected devices with their latest location. The gray dots imply that iCloud is trying to get the device's location or that it can't be located. Click on any dot in order to know which device it is.

You can click on **All Devices** on the middle-top side of the window to see the list of all your devices. Since Apple still uses Google Maps for Find My iPhone, you can zoom in or change its map type to the **Satellite** or **Hybrid** view.

Send a sound alert to devices

With Find My iPhone, you can send a sound alert to your devices. So, if your device is missing somewhere in your room, you can find it just by hearing the sound alert you've sent, by performing the following steps:

1. On the map, click on the dot that represents the device you want to send an alert to. Click on the **i** button beside it.

2. A device info dialog will appear. Click on the **Play Sound** button.

3. Then, a banner with a sound alert appears on the device. An e-mail confirmation is also sent to your iCloud e-mail address.

Remotely lock your device with Lost Mode

While your Mac/iOS device is in the Lost Mode, you can set up a passcode and lock it remotely. So, the device will ask to enter the passcode for unlocking your Mac/iOS device. To remotely lock your device from your another Mac/ iOS device, you need to perform the following instructions:

1. On the map, click on the dot that represents the device you want to remotely lock. Click on the **i** button beside it.

2. A device info dialog will appear. Click on the **Lost Mode** button.

3. Enter a phone number where you can be reached. It's really useful when your device is lost. Click on **Next**.

4. Enter a personalized message that will be shown on your device's screen. You might be asked for a four-digit passcode for your lost iPhone. If you've set a passcode before, your iPhone will be locked with the same passcode. Click on **Done**.

Your device is immediately locked, and a confirmation e-mail is sent to iCloud Mail to tell you that Lost Mode has been activated on your device. Once you find your device, unlock it with your four-digit code or passcode and Lost Mode will be disabled automatically.

Remotely wipe your device

If you have lost your Mac/iOS device or it has been stolen and you have lots of important data on it, it's better for you to remotely wipe it all. To remotely wipe data from your Mac/device, you need to perform the following steps:

1. On the map, click on the dot that represents the device you want to remotely wipe. Click on the **i** button beside it.

2. A device info dialog will appear. Click on the **Erase iPhone**, **Erase iPad**, **Erase iPod touch**, or **Erase Mac** button.

3. Then, a confirmation dialog button will appear. If you're sure you want to remotely wipe your device, enter your iCloud account / Apple ID password and click on **Erase**.

4. Your device is remotely wiped immediately. If the device is not connected to the Internet, it's going to be wiped immediately once it gets connected to the Internet.

iWork for iCloud (beta)

In the previous chapter, we discussed iWork and how it collaborates with iCloud. In the latest version of iWork for Mac and iOS, you can save iWork documents and store them to the iCloud server. It's really good if you're working on a document on multiple devices. However, now you can also create a new document directly from the web browser with iWork for iCloud. When this book was being written, Apple had a beta release of iWork for iCloud.

Just like the iWork suite on Mac or iOS, there are three apps on iCloud: Pages, Keynote, and Numbers. Click on one of the three apps' icons on the `iCloud.com` home screen. You can see all of your stored documents for this iWork app on `iCloud.com`. You can start to create a new document by clicking on **Create Document** with a big plus icon. You can also download any uploaded documents in the iWork document type, Microsoft Office document type, or PDF, as well as upload, duplicate, or delete any document. Remember: once you delete a document, it's going to disappear from every single iWork app.

Pages for iCloud

On Pages for iCloud, you can create a new document from the blank or selected templates provided by Apple. You will get exactly the same templates on Pages for Mac and Pages for iOS. After you choose a template, the Pages workspace appears as a new browser window.

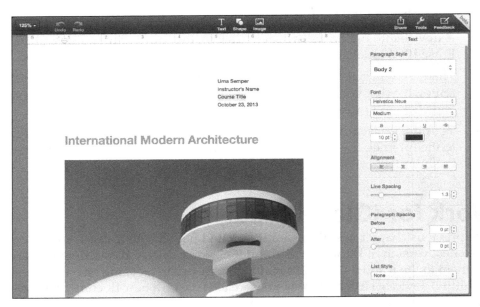

On the Pages for iCloud workspace, you will see a similar interface like that of Pages for iOS. There are toolbars at the top of the window of the document you're working on, and the **Text** sidebar on the right-hand side. It can mostly do everything you can do on the Mac or iOS version of the app.

After you finish the document, you can directly send the document as a Pages, Microsoft Word, or PDF document from your iCloud Mail account. There's no need to save the document, as iCloud will do it automatically for you.

Keynote for iCloud

On Keynote for iCloud, you can create a new presentation from the blank or selected templates provided by Apple. You will also get exactly the same templates on Keynote for Mac and iOS. After you choose a template, the Keynote workspace appears as a new browser window.

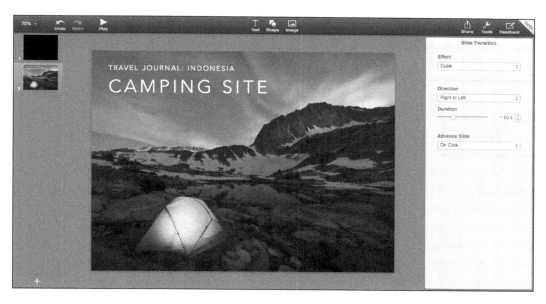

On the Keynote for iCloud workspace, you see a similar interface like that of Keynote for iOS. There are toolbars at the top of the window of the document you're working on, and a formatting sidebar on the right-hand side. It can do mostly everything you can do on the Mac or iOS version of the app, including playing your presentation with well-known sophisticated transitions inside the web browser.

After you finish the document, you can directly send the document as a Keynote, Microsoft PowerPoint, or PDF document from your iCloud Mail account. There's no need to save the document, as iCloud will do it automatically for you.

Numbers for iCloud

On Numbers for iCloud, you can create a new spreadsheet from the blank or selected templates provided by Apple. Just like its counterparts, you will get exactly the same templates that you get on Numbers for Mac and Numbers for iOS. After you choose a template, the Numbers workspace appears as a new browser window.

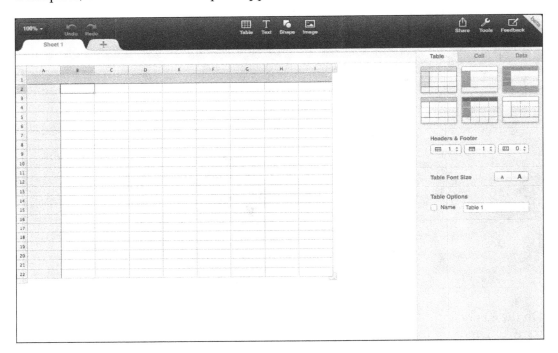

On the Numbers for iCloud workspace, you will see a similar interface like that of Numbers for iOS. There are toolbars at the top of the window of the document you're working on, and the **Table**, **Cell**, and **Data** sidebar is on the right-hand side. It can do mostly everything you can do on the Mac or iOS version of the app except for entering formulas.

After you finish the document, you can directly send the document as a Pages, Microsoft Excel, or PDF document from your iCloud Mail account. There's no need to save the document, as iCloud will do it automatically for you.

Find My Friends

Find My Friends is a new iOS app that lets you find your friends immediately using Location Services. You can locate your friends as long as they approve it and give iCloud the permission to locate them for you.

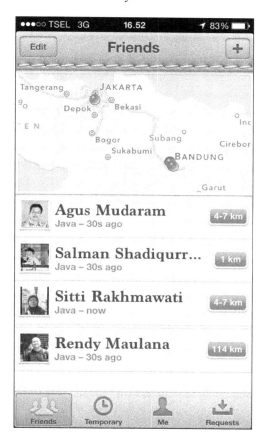

There are two ways to locate your friends; you can locate them permanently as long as they give you permission, or you could invite your friends to locate them temporarily based on a period of time. After the period has expired, your friends' locations disappear automatically.

Find My Friends requires iOS 5 or later, and you need to download the free app on the App Store. Unlike any other feature on iCloud, you can only use the service with the native app and not from iCloud.com.

To permanently add a contact, tap on the **+** button on the top right-hand corner and enter your friend's Apple ID in the **To** field. You can enter a personal message and tap the **Send** button to send the request. Once your friend has accepted you request, you can locate him or her.

To temporarily add a contact, tap on **Temporary** and then on the **+** button on the top right-hand corner. Enter your friend's Apple ID, name event of the invitation, and set the time when this location tracking has to stop. Tap on **Send** to send the requests.

Summary

With iCloud.com, you can access most of the iCloud services everywhere using a web browser. It's really useful if you need to check e-mails or to-do lists if you have left all of your stuff at home. So far, there are only seven web apps available on iCloud.com. Apple also adds the iWork for iCloud web apps, including Pages, Numbers, and Keynote. So, you're not only seeing the documents but also editing or creating new ones directly from iCloud.com.

8
Backing Up Devices to iCloud

Along with other features and services, iCloud allows you to back up your iOS devices directly to the cloud. You can also restore them directly from iCloud. Since your iOS device directly interacts with iCloud, there's no computer needed to activate and use this feature. It's what Apple calls the *PC-free* feature.

Understanding iCloud Backup

Before iCloud, users needed to plug in their iOS devices to the computer just for backing up devices via USB cable. iTunes helps you to back up data on your device, for example, contacts, purchased content, photos and videos in Camera Roll, and all your personal configurations. iTunes also helps you restore the previous backup to the device.

Now, PC-free (introduced in iOS 5) and iCloud features eliminate the need to use a USB cable in order to backup and restore. Since PC-free eliminates the need to use a cable to back up and restore your devices to the computer, for which you can just use a Wi-Fi connection, iCloud lets you do backup and restoration to the cloud using any connection available, anytime and anywhere. With the free 5 GB storage on iCloud, you can use it to store your iOS device's backup contents. Even now you can back up your device to iCloud, it's still possible to perform a local backup process with iTunes.

Before going through on how to back up, you need to know what content will be backed up to iCloud. Some of your device's content will consume iCloud storage and some won't. Here's what iCloud backs up that will be counted in iCloud storage usage:

- All photos and videos in Camera Roll.
- Ringtones, including the assigned tones configured for your contacts.
- Device settings, such as accounts settings, lists of installed apps, home screen configuration (including folders configuration).
- Depending on the app, an app may store data to designated sandboxed folders. This data will be backed up to iCloud.
- All conversations on Messages: iMessage, SMS, MMS, and Visual Voicemail (if your carrier supports it).

The following content backed up to iCloud but not considered in iCloud storage usage, hence, they don't reduce the remaining space of your iCloud storage:

- All purchased content from the iTunes Store, including music, movies, ringtones, books, TV shows, and apps. This content is already covered by iTunes in the Cloud service.
- All pictures that are uploaded to Photo Stream.

iCloud doesn't back up the following items:

- All multimedia content not purchased from the iTunes Store
- Photos that were synced from local iPhoto Library on your computer
- Podcasts and audio books

Using iCloud to back up or restore an iOS device

To back up an iOS device to iCloud, you can turn it ON directly from the device or you can enable it from the iTunes Store. iCloud automatically backs up your device when it's connected to any Wi-Fi connection, a power source, and when the screen is locked.

Turning ON iCloud Backup on iOS devices

To enable iCloud to back up an iOS device from the device, follow the given steps:

1. Navigate to **Settings | iCloud | Storage & Backup**.
2. To enable it, set the **iCloud Backup** toggle to the ON position.

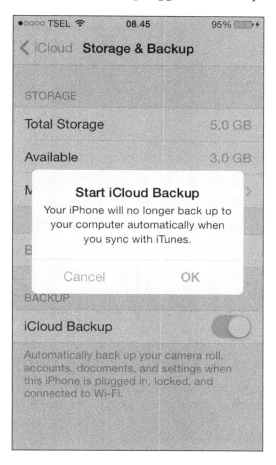

3. iOS asks for your confirmation to enable iCloud Backup for the device and it will no longer back up to your computer when you sync it with iTunes.
4. Tap on **Back Up Now** to perform iCloud Backup manually.

Turning ON iCloud Backup from iTunes

If you connect your device to iTunes (via a USB cable or Wi-Fi), you can enable iCloud Backup from iTunes, as shown in the following screenshot:

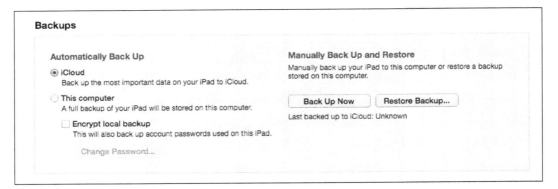

1. Connect your iOS device to your Mac or PC and launch iTunes.

2. On iTunes 11, click on your iOS device at the right corner of the window.

3. On your device's overview, click on the iCloud radio button in the **Automatically Backup** section.

 When you're performing your first iCloud Backup, it may take a while depending on how big your device's backup content is. After that, iCloud only backs up the changes, hence, it will be faster.

Restoring an iOS device from iCloud

Restoring an iOS device to its previous/original state is an easy task, and personally, I think it's by far the easiest in comparison to other mobile platforms. When you're restoring an iOS device via a personal computer, iTunes handles everything from restoring device information to all your backed-up content, including messages, pictures and videos on Camera Roll.

With iCloud, the process is quite similar to that of iTunes but it happens wirelessly via a Wi-Fi connection. You can restore an iOS device with iCloud on any device running iOS 5 or later versions.

To restore an iOS device from an iCloud Backup, the following steps need to be performed:

1. Erase all content on your iOS device first. Navigate to **Settings | General | Reset**, then tap on **Erase All Content and Settings**. Tap on **Erase** to confirm the process.

2. Once it's erased, follow the instructions on the setup assistant until you see the **Set Up** (with device name) screen. Tap on **Restore from iCloud Backup** to restore your iOS device using iCloud Backup.

3. The next screen shows the recent iCloud backups for you to choose. Choose one of them and then tap on **Restore**. Your device will download the backup from the iCloud server and the restoration begins.

iCloud storage plans

As mentioned before, every iCloud user gets 5 GB of storage for free. You can see how much storage you've used, what data is stored on iCloud, and also upgrade your current storage plan to a higher one from the iCloud preference pane on Mac, iCloud settings on iOS, or iCloud Control Panel on Windows PC. You're also allowed to downgrade your current storage plan if you've upgraded it before.

Managing iCloud storage on iOS

In iOS, you can manage your iCloud storage and see the list of all documents that are already uploaded to iCloud. You can also delete any iOS device's backup or documents that you want to. The following instructions show you how to do this:

1. Navigate to **Settings | iCloud | Storage & Backup**.

2. On the **Storage & Backup** screen, you can see your current total iCloud storage and how much storage is available to be used. Tap on **Manage Storage** to manage your storage.

3. On the **Manage Storage** screen, you can see all of the backups and data stored by apps. Tap any app name and see what kind of app data is stored in your iCloud storage.

4. If you want to delete the app data, navigate to **Edit** | **Delete All**, or if you want to delete individually, tap on the **Edit** | stop icon on the left-hand side | **Delete** on the right side.

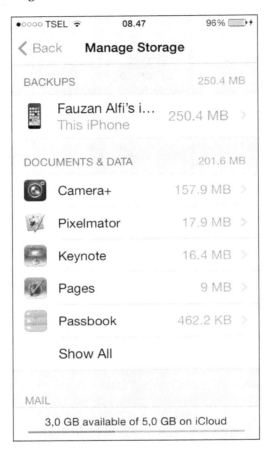

Managing iCloud storage on Mac

You can also manage your iCloud storage from a Mac and see the list of all documents that are already uploaded to iCloud. You can delete some or all of the documents that you want to. The following steps show you how to do this:

1. Navigate to **System Preferences** | **iCloud** | **Manage**.

2. A new window shows all of the data stored on your iCloud storage. Click on any app to see more details.

3. To delete a document or data, click on one of them and then click on **Delete**. If you want to delete all of the stored documents or the data of an app, click on **Delete All**.

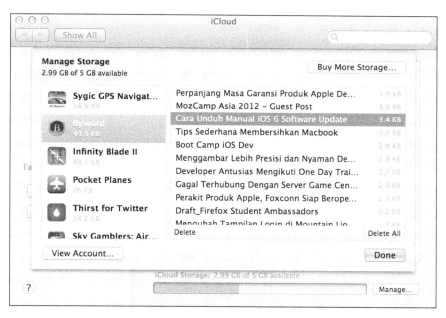

Changing storage plan on iOS

For some people, 5 GB of iCloud storage is not enough. You can change or even upgrade your storage plan to a higher one on your iOS device. You'll be charged immediately each year until you cancel your plan or change it to the free 5 GB tier. The following steps show you how to change your storage plan on iOS:

1. Navigate to **Settings** | **iCloud** | **Storage & Backup** | **Change Storage Plan**.

2. On the **Buy More Storage** screen, you can see your current iCloud storage plan. To upgrade to a recommended higher plan, tap the plan under **Choose an Upgrade** label.

3. To downgrade your storage plan, tap on **Downgrade Options** and enter your Apple ID credentials.

4. Tap on any lower plan to downgrade your iCloud storage plan. Then, tap on **Done**.

Changing storage plan on Mac

Just like in iOS, you can also change or even upgrade your storage plan to a bigger one on your Mac. The following steps show you how to change your storage plan on Mac:

1. Navigate to **System Preferences | iCloud | Manage | Change Storage Plan**.

2. A new window will display your current plan. To upgrade to a higher plan, click on the plan under the **Choose an Upgrade** label, as shown in the following screenshot:

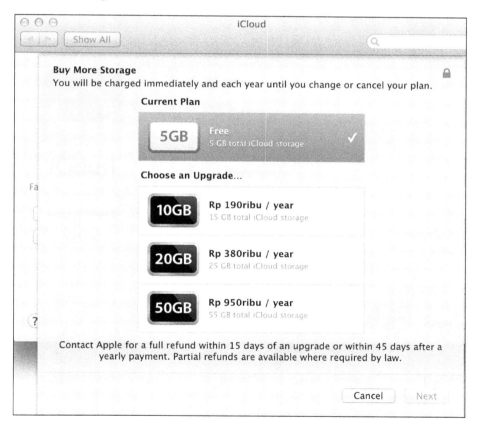

3. To downgrade your storage plan, click on **Downgrade Options** and enter your Apple ID credentials.

4. Click on any lower plan to downgrade your iCloud storage plan. Then, click on **Done**.

Summary

Backing up a device is an essential thing to do for every computer and/or smartphone user. You won't lose data if your device is lost or you accidentally delete files. With iCloud Backup, you can back up your device every time and everywhere without a computer. If you have access to a fast and stable Internet connection, you might find no problem in backing up your devices daily. If not, it will take hours or even days depending on your device's storage and it's better if you perform a local backup using iTunes.

Using iCloud with OS X

9

Since the release of OS X Mountain Lion, Apple deeply integrates iCloud with OS X. Most apps, including stock apps, are connected and integrated with iCloud services. Even on the first boot, a user will be asked for his or her Apple ID (if he or she has one), or to create a new one to activate iCloud on Mac.

iCloud-enabled Mac apps

On OS X, most stock apps such as Mail, Contacts, Calendar, and Notes are integrated with iCloud. However, only few of them are available on OS X and they sync between your Mac computers. Just like other apps, an app's documents are uploaded to iCloud server and then automatically shared to the other available devices.

Preview

Preview is the easiest way to preview image files and PDF documents on your Mac. You can also easily edit or annotate them. On OS X Mountain Lion, you can store the documents supported by Preview on the iCloud server directly from the Preview app.

When you launch Preview, a new window appears like the one shown in the following screenshot. It shows **iCloud for Preview**. You can move your existing documents that are supported by Preview just by dragging them to the window.

All dragged documents are automatically stored on iCloud under the Preview app. You also can share any stored document with Mail or other apps on your Mac.

TextEdit

TextEdit is the simplest way to create a document file and open any document files, including Microsoft Office type documents on your Mac. It looks like an ordinary text editor but actually you can use TextEdit as your primary word processing app.

Just like Preview, a new window appears when you launch TextEdit, as shown in the following screenshot. It shows **iCloud for TextEdit**. You can move your existing documents that are supported by TextEdit just by dragging them to the window. All dragged documents are automatically stored on iCloud under the TextEdit app. You also can share any stored document with Mail or other apps on your Mac.

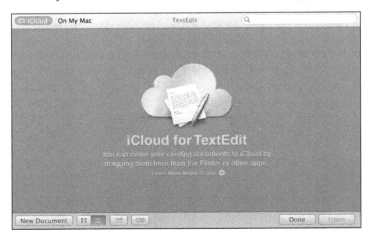

iWork for Mac

In the previous chapters, we learned about iWork and how the apps work seamlessly with your Mac and iOS. You can browse all of your stored iWork documents not only from iWork for iCloud, or iWork for iOS, but also directly from iWork for Mac, including Pages, Numbers, and Keynote.

When you start any iWork app, a new iCloud window appears. You can see all stored documents depending on which iWork app you select. If you select Pages, you can only see all Pages documents. Before you use this feature, make sure that you've upgraded your iWork for Mac apps to the latest version from Software Update or Mac App Store.

Back to My Mac

Another cool feature on iCloud for Mac users is Back to My Mac. It lets you connect your Mac to another Mac, or AirPort Disk, or Time Capsule, which is located somewhere else, when connected to the Internet. In the past, it was really hard to get this thing to work. It had to be configured manually and everything was technical. Apple is simplifying the procedure with its Back to My Mac feature so that users can connect their Macs at their office to their Macs at home, securely and easily without any hassle.

Once you activate this feature, both your Mac and the other Mac are connected in a local network. Since it's connected over the Internet, the transfer rate is going to be a little slower, unlike when they are connected on a local network at home or the office.

With Back to My Mac on your Mac, there are three things you can do:

- **File Sharing**: You can connect to a remote Mac, mount any drives in it, and copy files from your Mac to a remote Mac directly from Finder. If you have any storage connected to an Airport Base Station or Time Capsule, you can also mount it and copy any files from Finder. To make this possible, make sure that your remote Mac is connected to the Internet and your AirPort Base Station or Time Capsule is connected with the same network as the remote Mac.

- **Screen Sharing**: You can see what a remote Mac's display shows and also control it directly from your Mac. All things you can do with your remote Mac are just the same as controlling your Mac, including launching apps, taking screenshots, or copying files.

- **Remote Airport Configuration**: You can also change any settings on a remote AirPort Base Station or Time Capsule using AirPort Utility.

 For more information, you can visit `http://www.apple.com/support/icloud/back-to-my-mac/`.

System requirements

To make sure that you can connect with your remote Mac using Back to My Mac, there are some basic requirements:

- An iCloud account.

- A broadband Internet connection.

- Two or more Mac computers with OS X 10.5.8 or higher, and each of them are configured with the same iCloud account.

- It is recommended to use a Time Capsule or AirPort Base Station on your home network.

- A router that fully supports either NAT Port Mapping Protocol (NAT-PMP) or Universal Plug and Play (UPnP). Ask your administrator or router manufacturer to make sure that your router supports it.

Setting up Back to My Mac on your Mac

To use Back to My Mac, you need to activate it on both your host Mac and your remote Mac.

Activating Back to My Mac is very simple. The following instructions will help you to activate this feature on your Mac:

1. Make sure that your Mac is using the latest version of OS X. Navigate to **Apple Menu | Software Update** to install the necessary updates.

2. Navigate to **System Preferences | iCloud**.

3. Click on the **Back to My Mac** checkbox to enable the feature on your Mac. iCloud is going to check your Mac and its Internet connection to see if it's ready for Back to My Mac or not.

4. If something goes wrong while activating Back to My Mac, you can click on **More** on the left side of the pane to see the problem and its solution.

5. Go back to **System Preferences** and click on **Sharing**.

6. Click on the **File Sharing** checkbox to share files with the remote Mac. Also, click on the **Screen Sharing** checkbox to share your Mac's screen and see the remote Mac's shared screen.

If you're using any AirPort Base Station or Time Capsule, you can set your Mac to automatically wake when you want to use it remotely using Back to My Mac. It's called **Wake on Demand**. The following steps show you how to activate it:

1. First, navigate to **System Preferences** | **Energy Saver**.

2. Click on the **Power Adapter** button.

3. Check the **Wake for Network access, Wake for Ethernet network access**, or **Wake for Wi-Fi network access** checkbox. Then, click on **OK**.

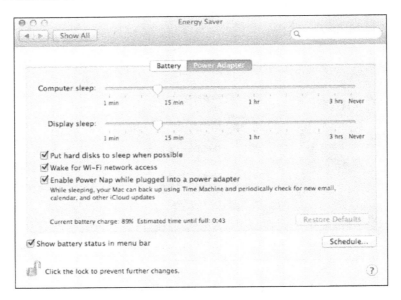

Configuring your router

Before we can use Back to My Mac, you need to configure your router to make it work properly with this feature. It's much better if your router is an AirPort Base Station or Time Capsule. For those who have an AirPort Base Station (AirPort Express or AirPort Extreme) or Time Capsule, the following instructions show you how to configure the router:

1. Navigate to **Applications | Utilities | AirPort Utility**.
2. Select your AirPort Base Station and click on **Edit**.
3. Navigate to **Network | Network Options**.
4. Check the **Enable NAT Port Mapping Protocol** checkbox. Then, click on **Save and Update** to make the changes in your selected AirPort Base Station or Time Capsule.

If you're using any other third-party router, ask your router's manufacturer for more information on enabling NAT-PMP or UPnP on the router.

Using Back to My Mac

After you set up both your host Mac and remote Mac with a router, you can use Back to My Mac. All you need to do is open a Finder window. Finder shows all of the remote Mac computers that you've configured before, Time Capsule, or any AirPort Disk in the sidebar.

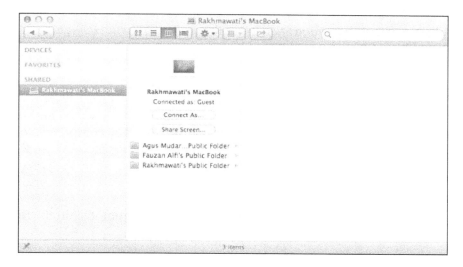

Remote file sharing

With Remote file sharing, you can drag any files from your remote Mac, Time Capsule, or hard disk to your host Mac, or drag any files from your host Mac to your remote Mac. You can do everything that you do on your own local storage drive. Everything happens only in the Finder on your Mac. To use Remote File Sharing, the following steps need to be performed:

1. Open the Finder window.

2. Find the Mac computer that you want to connect to remotely in the **Shared** section on the sidebar.

3. Click on **Connect As** to connect to a remote Mac. You can connect to it as a guest, a registered available user on the remote Mac, or using an Apple ID.

4. Choose one of the options and enter the credential.

5. Once it's connected, you can browse shared drive on the remote Mac.

Remote screen sharing

With Remote screen sharing, you can control your remote Mac's screen and anything you want to do just like the way in which you control a normal computer. You can open applications, files, or even take screenshots of the remote Mac. To use Remote Screen Sharing, the following steps need to be performed:

1. Open the Finder window.

2. Find the Mac computer that you want to connect to remotely in the **Shared** section on the sidebar.

3. Click on **Share Screen** to connect to a remote Mac. You can connect to it as a registered available user on the remote Mac or using an Apple ID.

4. Choose one of the options and enter the credential.

5. Once it's connected, you can control the remote Mac's screen.

Summary

On OS X, we can do a lot of things with iCloud, such as saving files to iCloud servers directly from apps, or even accessing the other Mac using the Back to my Mac feature. Since they're developed together by Apple, you won't find any difficulties in using Back to my Mac. In the next chapter, we will learn how to integrate iCloud with Windows PC and how good their relationship is.

10

Using iCloud with Windows

Not only for OS X or iOS, iCloud also supports PC running Windows. Since the release of iTunes in 2003, Apple has been creating its homemade applications for Windows. For its online service, Apple initially deployed MobileMe, and supported Windows by creating a MobileMe Control Panel.

After MobileMe was discontinued, iCloud took its place as the main online service and Apple released iCloud Control Panel for Windows as well. This way, iOS users do not have to own a Mac in order to sync their content to their computer. They can do it with Windows by installing the iCloud Control Panel for Windows.

However, not all iCloud services are available on Windows; for example, OS X services such as Notes, Documents, and Data, and other Mac-specific services such as Find My Mac and Back to My Mac are not available on Windows. The rest of this chapter will discuss iCloud features on Windows and how to configure them so that you can use them.

Configuring the iCloud Control Panel

Before we proceed to using iCloud services on Windows, we need to install the iCloud Control Panel. In *Chapter 2, Getting Started with iCloud*, we learned how to install iCloud Control Panel on Windows. In this chapter, we will learn how to configure iCloud so that it is usable on Windows.

Syncing bookmarks

On Mac OS X and iOS, iCloud syncs all bookmarks between the Safari web browser on each platform. On Windows, iCloud supports bookmarks syncing with Internet Explorer, Firefox, and Chrome. Apple does not support this feature on its own browser, Safari for Windows, since it was discontinued in May 2012. Firefox and Chrome support were added in mid-2013 and require an add-on or plugin for each browser.

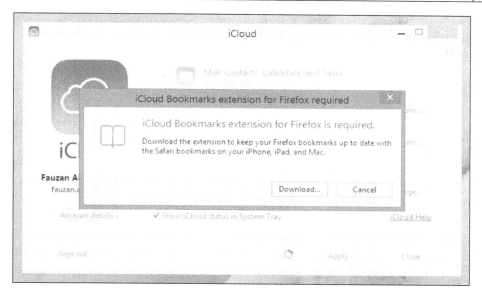

To activate iCloud bookmarks syncing, open iCloud Control Panel and click on the **Bookmarks** checkbox to activate. iCloud will ask which browser you want to sync with. You can choose more than one browser if you have Internet Explorer, Firefox, and/or Chrome already installed on your PC. Then, iCloud prompts you to download an add-on/plugin for Firefox and Chrome if you haven't installed it already.

After installing the add-on/plugin, iCloud automatically syncs all of your stored bookmarks to your selected browser and stores any new bookmarks from your current browser back to iCloud. For Internet Explorer 10 or later (available on Windows 8 or later), you can see all of your bookmarks (or favorite sites) by pressing *Alt+C*.

Integrating Photo Stream with file explorer

In iOS, all pictures taken are automatically uploaded to Photo Stream and you can see them on the Photo Stream tab of the Photos app on iOS. In Mac OS X, you need iPhoto to see and store photos to Photo Stream and share them with Shared Photo Stream. In Windows, Photo Stream is integrated with File Explorer of Windows 8 (or Windows Explorer on earlier versions of Windows).

To activate Photo Stream, open the iCloud Control Panel and click on the **Photos** checkbox. Then, iCloud automatically downloads all of your stored photos both on Photo Stream and Shared Photo Stream. Then, you can see all of the synced photos in File Explorer by clicking on **iCloud Photos** on the left sidebar under the **Favorites** section.

Managing iCloud storage

To manage iCloud Storage on Windows, perform the following steps:

1. Open the iCloud Control Panel.

2. Inside the **iCloud Storage** box, click on **Manage**.

3. Then, the **iCloud Storage** window is displayed. You can see the list of apps that store data on your iCloud account. Just as in Mac OS X, you can manually delete a document or all of them.

4. If you want to upgrade or downgrade your iCloud storage plan, click on **Change Storage Plan** on the top right-hand corner. A new window appears along with a desired storage plan.

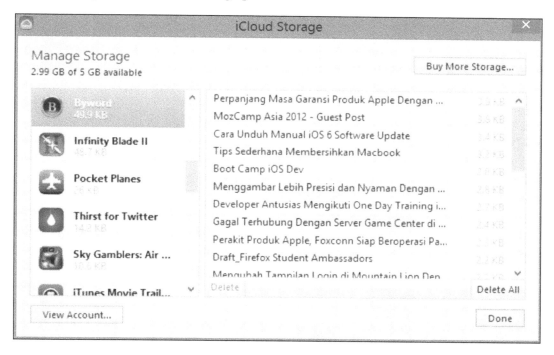

Managing an iCloud account

To manage an iCloud account on Windows, perform the following steps:

1. Open iCloud Control Panel.

2. Click on **Account details...** on the left-hand side of the window.

3. Click on **Manage Apple ID** to redirect you to the Apple ID website.

iCloud and Microsoft Outlook

For Mac OS X and iOS, iCloud will sync productivity content between similar apps, such as Mail, Contacts, Calendar, and Reminders. In Windows, content can be synced to only one app: Microsoft Office Outlook. You need Microsoft Outlook 2007 or later to sync with iCloud.

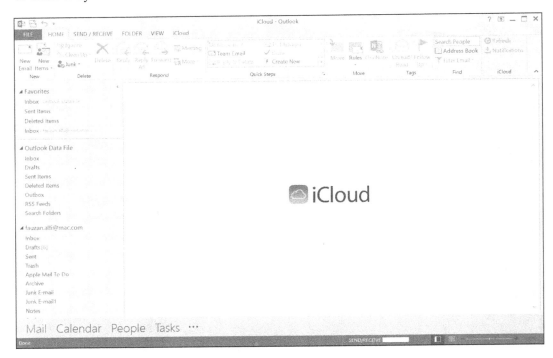

Configuring Mail, Contacts, Calendar, and Reminders on Outlook

To access Mail, Contacts, Calendar, and Reminders on Outlook, perform the following steps:

1. Make sure that any supported version of Microsoft Outlook is installed on your Windows computer or Mac computer running Windows.

2. Open Outlook for the first time. Outlook will create a profile later iCloud is able to detect later and configure for you.

3. Open iCloud Control Panel.

4. Click on the **Mail, Contacts, Calendar and Tasks** checkbox to activate these services.

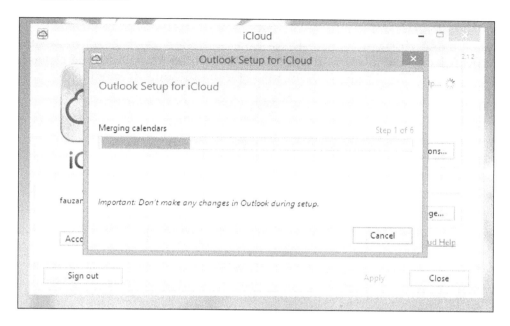

5. iCloud will search the Outlook profile to configure. After that, iCloud starts to configure the iCloud Mail IMAP settings, download all contacts, calendar, and reminders data. It's important not to open or make changes in Outlook during this process.

6. Once it's done, enter your iCloud account password if you are asked. Then, enjoy the configured Outlook with iCloud.

Now, you can access your iCloud Mail, Contacts, Calendar, and Reminders directly from Microsoft Outlook. You can also see the new **iCloud** tab on the Outlook's ribbon menu.

Accessing Mail, Contacts, Calendar, and Reminders on Outlook

Outlook 2013 is used for demonstration purpose in this book. To access iCloud Mail, Contacts, Calendar, and Reminders in Outlook, you just pick one of the labels that represent the services you want to access from the bottom left-hand side of Outlook. You can click on **Mail** to see your iCloud Mail, **Calendar** for your iCloud Calendar, **People** for your iCloud Contacts, and **Tasks** for your iCloud Reminders.

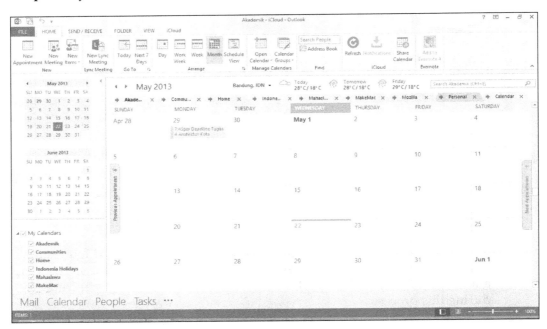

Summary

With iCloud Control Panel, Apple lets you use iCloud services even when you're not using OS X and only have a PC running the Windows operating system on it. iCloud Control Panel can also be installed in the Boot Camp installation on your Mac. Unlike Mac, you must buy Microsoft Outlook to access your iCloud Mail, Contacts, Calendar, and Tasks from a Windows PC. However, you can still access your Photo Streams from File Explorer / Windows Explorer and bookmarks from Internet Explorer. Apple limits iCloud integration on Windows. The best way to get better iCloud experiences and integration is to use a Mac computer.

Index

Platform as a Service (PaaS) 14
Play Sound button 103
Power Adapter button 126
preview 121
purchased movies
  on Apple TV 76
purchased music
  on Apple TV 76
Purchased tab 94

R

reminders
  about 61
  accessing, on Outlook 138
  configuring, on Outlook 136, 137
  on iCloud.com 63
  on iOS devices 61, 62
  on Mac 62
remote file sharing 128
remote screen sharing 128, 129

S

Safari web browser
  about 87
  bookmarks, syncing 90
  iCloud Tabs, syncing between devices 91, 92
  Reading List, syncing 92
  sync for Safari on iOS, enabling 87
  sync for Safari on Mac, enabling 89
Save to Camera Roll icon 67
Send button 57
Sent folder 37
Settings | iCloud 26
Share button 47
Share Location button 57
Short Message Service. *See* SMS
SMS
  about 49
  versus iMessage 50
storage plan
  changing, on iOS 118, 119
  changing, on Mac 119, 120

T

TextEdit 122
texts
  sending 56

W

Wake on Demand 126
Worldwide Developer Conference 2013 9

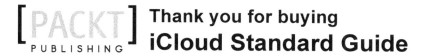

About Packt Publishing

Packt, pronounced 'packed', published its first book *"Mastering phpMyAdmin for Effective MySQL Management"* in April 2004 and subsequently continued to specialize in publishing highly focused books on specific technologies and solutions.

Our books and publications share the experiences of your fellow IT professionals in adapting and customizing today's systems, applications, and frameworks. Our solution based books give you the knowledge and power to customize the software and technologies you're using to get the job done. Packt books are more specific and less general than the IT books you have seen in the past. Our unique business model allows us to bring you more focused information, giving you more of what you need to know, and less of what you don't.

Packt is a modern, yet unique publishing company, which focuses on producing quality, cutting-edge books for communities of developers, administrators, and newbies alike. For more information, please visit our website: www.packtpub.com.

Writing for Packt

We welcome all inquiries from people who are interested in authoring. Book proposals should be sent to author@packtpub.com. If your book idea is still at an early stage and you would like to discuss it first before writing a formal book proposal, contact us; one of our commissioning editors will get in touch with you.

We're not just looking for published authors; if you have strong technical skills but no writing experience, our experienced editors can help you develop a writing career, or simply get some additional reward for your expertise.

Mastering Apple Aperture

ISBN: 978-1-84969-356-1   Paperback: 264 pages

Master the art of enhancing, organizing, exporting, and printing your photos using Apple's Aperture

1. Learn how to use the advanced features of Apple Aperture.

2. Become well-versed with advanced topics such as curves and how raw conversion works.

3. Written in an easy-to-follow conversational style and packed with tips and tricks for optimizing your workflow.

Instant Apple iBooks How-to [Instant]

ISBN: 978-1-84969-402-5   Paperback: 52 pages

Learn how to read and write books for iBookstore, by fully utilizing Apple iBooks and iBooks Author

1. Learn something new in an Instant! A short, fast, focused guide delivering immediate results.

2. Learn everything you need know, from reading iBooks to creating and publishing your own.

3. Best practices and solutions for Apple iBooks.

4. Presented in an easy-to-follow tutorial style, this book is your quick and compact guide to iBooks.

Apple Motion 5 Cookbook

ISBN: 978-1-84969-380-6   Paperback: 416 pages

Over 110 recipes to build simple and complex motion graphics in the blink of an eye

1. Easy to follow, hands-on instructions that simplify the learning process.

2. Lots of in-depth information for FCPX users looking to integrate more motion graphics into their projects.

3. Learn keyboard shortcuts that will save you hours and navigate Motion's interface like an expert.

iPad Enterprise Application Development BluePrints

ISBN: 978-1-84968-294-7   Paperback: 430 pages

Design and build your own enterprise applications for the iPad

1. Learn how to go about developing some simple, yet powerful applications with ease.

2. Each chapter explains about the technology in-depth, while providing you with enough information and examples to help grasp the technology.

3. Get to grips with integrating Facebook, iCloud, Twitter and Airplay into your applications.

4. Lots of step-by-step examples with images and diagrams to get you up to speed in no time, with helpful hints along the way.

www.ingramcontent.com/pod-product-compliance
Lightning Source LLC
Chambersburg PA
CBHW082119070326
40690CB00049B/3976